THE HOLOCAUST

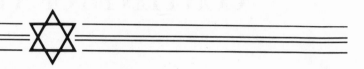

Selected Documents in Eighteen Volumes

John Mendelsohn
EDITOR

Donald S. Detwiler
ADVISORY EDITOR

A GARLAND SERIES

CONTENTS OF THE SERIES

THE HOLOCAUST

12. The "Final Solution" in the Extermination Camps and the Aftermath

Introduction by
Henry Friedlander

GARLAND PUBLISHING, INC.
NEW YORK · LONDON
1982

These documents have been reproduced from copies in
the National Archives. Dr. Mendelsohn's work was carried out entirely on his own time and without endorse-
ment or official participation by the National Archives as
an agency.

Library of Congress Cataloging in Publication Data
Main entry under title:

The "Final solution" in the extermination camps and
the aftermath.

(The Holocaust ; 12)
1. Holocaust, Jewish (1939–1945)—Sources.
I. Series: Holocaust ; 12.
D810.J4H655   vol. 12   940.53′15′03924s   81-80320
ISBN 0-8240-4886-5   [940.53′15′03924]   AACR2

Design by Jonathan Billing

The volumes in this series have been printed on acid-free,
250-year-life paper.

Printed in the United States of America

ACKNOWLEDGMENTS

I owe a debt of gratitude to many people who aided me during various stages of preparing these eighteen volumes. Of these I would like to mention by name a few without whose generous efforts this publication would have been impossible. I would like to thank Donald B. Schewe of the Franklin D. Roosevelt Library in Hyde Park, New York, for his speedy and effective help. Sally Marcks and Richard Gould of the Diplomatic Branch of the National Archives in Washington, D.C., extended help beyond their normal archival duties, as did Timothy Mulligan and George Wagner from the Modern Military Branch. Edward J. McCarter in the Still Picture Branch helped a great deal. I would also like to thank my wife, Tish, for letting me spend my evenings during the past few years with these volumes rather than with her and our children, Michael and Lisa.

J. M.

CONCENTRATION CAMPS

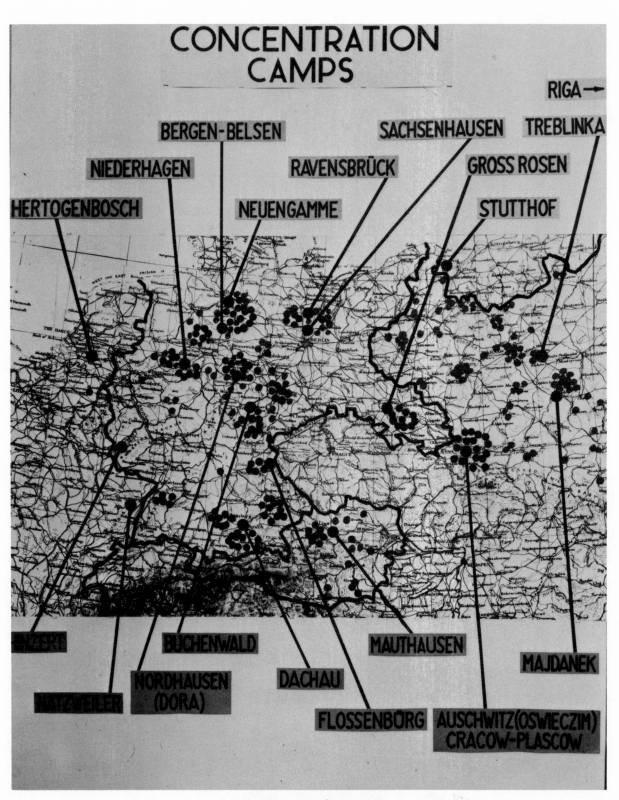

Map of concentration camps
International Military Tribunal
National Archives Record Group 238

INTRODUCTION

In 1941 Hitler ordered the physical destruction of the European Jews. Himmler and his SS—supported by party, army, government, and industry—had to implement this "Final Solution." The invasion of the Soviet Union provided the first opportunity for the practice of mass murder. In the newly occupied Russian territories mobile killing units, the SS *Einsatzgruppen*, simply rounded up and shot all Jews. But this method did not prove satisfactory. Mass executions were too public; the use of guns to kill multitudes imposed an unacceptable psychological burden on the executioners. The SS searched for a more efficient method; they found their answer in the killing centers, where they applied industrial techniques to the murder of the Jews.

The institution of the killing centers, where the victims were murdered in gas chambers, developed from two earlier experiments in mass murder. First, in 1939 the Führer Chancellery instituted the so-called euthanasia program, which provided for the killing of German nationals confined in mental institutions. The victims, selected by committees of physicians, were killed in specially constructed gas chambers. Second, in 1941 the technical department of the Central Office for Reich Security (RSHA) developed gas vans for the *Einsatzgruppen*; they were used in Russia—and at the Semlin camp in Serbia—to kill Jewish women and children.

The first killing center opened in Chelmno (Kulmhof) in December 1941. Located in the annexed territories of western Poland and supervised by the German governor in Posen, it was used to kill the Jews from Lodz and the smaller towns of the Wartheland. A primitive but highly efficient installation, Chelmno utilized gas vans to kill the arriving Jews. Operated by a special SS unit previously employed to kill mental patients in East Prussia, Chelmno was in operation during 1942 and again in the summer of 1944.

The Nazis perfected the technology of mass murder in three camps established early in 1942 in eastern Poland. The task of killing the Jews of Poland was assigned to Odilo Globocnik, the SS and police leader of Lublin, who coined the code name "Operation Reinhardt" for this enterprise. His office directed the roundups and the deportations to the camps; it also collected and transferred the confiscated Jewish properties. Globocnik founded three killing centers: Belzec, Sobibor, and Treblinka. The Führer Chancellery supplied and paid the German staff members, who were

The high-voltage fence surrounding a concentration camp
Miscellaneous materials of the Nuernberg Trials prosecution staff
National Archives Record Group 238

mostly men experienced in killing the mental patients; they were supported by units of Ukrainian volunteers, trained for this purpose at the SS camp Trawniki. To direct the three killing centers, Globocnik appointed Christian Wirth, a Stuttgart police officer previously employed in the euthanasia program.

Belzec, Sobibor, and Treblinka became extremely efficient killing centers. The victims arrived by train and were then "processed" on a kind of assembly line. They were first stripped of all belongings and were then driven naked into large chambers where they were killed by carbon monoxide gas; later their bodies were burned in large pits after all gold had been extracted from their teeth. These killing centers were not camps in the ordinary sense; the victims sent there were killed as soon as they arrived. Only a few victims were saved to perform the physical labor needed to run the camps, and eventually they were also killed. More than one and a half million Jews were murdered in the killing centers of Operation Reinhardt. Most came from central and eastern Poland, but a few also arrived from Russia, Slovakia, Germany, Holland, and France. The three killing centers were closed in the fall of 1943, two of them—Sobibor and Treblinka—after revolts by their Jewish inmates.

In Upper Silesia the SS constructed the largest and most efficient killing center. In 1940 they had built a regular concentration camp there; known as Auschwitz, it was originally designed to hold Polish political prisoners. In 1941 Himmler ordered the Auschwitz commandant Rudolf Hoess to develop facilities for the mass murder of the European Jews. Late in 1941 Hoess experimented by gassing Russian POW's; early in 1942 he perfected his methods by killing the Jews of Upper Silesia. Auschwitz was ready to receive its victims.

Hoess added a number of technological refinements to improve the system of mass murder. Dissatisfied with the use of carbon monoxide, he ended the dependence on motors to produce a deadly gas. Instead, he used crystallized prussic acid, a pesticide with the trade name Zyklon B. Eventually Hoess also eliminated the practice of burning the bodies in the open. Instead, the bodies were burned in four large crematoria, which also contained the gas chambers. Hoess located these killing installations in Birkenau, also known as Auschwitz II. More than two million victims were killed in Auschwitz-Birkenau; most of them were Jews from all parts of Europe, but some were gypsies, Russian POW's, and ill prisoners of all nationalities.

The Jews arrived in Auschwitz-Birkenau by train and were then "processed" by the method developed earlier in the other killing centers. But there was one important difference: not every victim was killed upon arrival. The killing center at Birkenau (and the smaller one at Maidanek near Lublin) was part of the concentration camp system operated by the SS Central Office for Economy and Administration (WVHA). The RSHA provided the victims; the WVHA disposed of them. But WVHA operated an economic empire that needed slave labor. Thus Auschwitz-Birkenau served a dual purpose: killing Jews and providing Jewish labor. Upon arrival of RSHA Jewish transports SS physicians "selected" those able to work; all others were immediately gassed.

A giant camp grew in Birkenau adjacent to the killing center to hold those selected for slave labor. After quarantine most were sent to the I. G. Farben complex Buna-Monowitz, also known as Auschwitz III, and to a large number of subsidiary camps. As the German war economy demanded increasing numbers of workers in 1943 and 1944, Jews selected for labor in Birkenau flooded all German camps, mingling with all other prisoners in the slave empire operated by WVHA. Millions perished, but a few thousand survived to be liberated by the Allied armies.

The documents reproduced in this volume come from the evidence collected for the international and United States trials at Nuernberg. They include the statistical compilation by the SS of the "Final Solution" up to 1943 (the so-called Korherr reports); the postwar interrogations of Auschwitz commandant Rudolf Hoess, Eichmann office member Dieter Wisliceny, and Himmler's economic negotiator Kurt Becher; correspondence dealing with Zyklon B, the gas used for killing in Auschwitz; and reports concerning Operation Reinhardt, the code name for the killing of the Jews in eastern Poland.

Henry Friedlander
Brooklyn College
City University of New York

SOURCE ABBREVIATIONS
AND DESCRIPTIONS

Nuernberg Document

Records from five of the twenty-five Nuernberg Trials prosecution document series: the NG (Nuernberg Government) series, the NI (Nuernberg Industrialist) series, the NO (Nuernberg Organizations) series, the NOKW (Nuernberg Armed Forces High Command) series, and the PS (Paris-Storey) series. Also included are such Nuernberg Trials prosecution records as interviews, interrogations, and affidavits, excerpts from the transcripts of the proceedings, briefs, judgments, and sentences. These records were used by the prosecution staff of the International Military Tribunal at Nuernberg or the twelve United States military tribunals there, and they are part of National Archives Record Group 238, National Archives Collection of World War II War Crimes Records.

OSS

Reports by the Office of Strategic Services in National Archives Record Group 226.

SEA

Staff Evidence Analysis: a description of documents used by the Nuernberg prosecution staff. Although the SEA's tended to describe only the evidentiary parts of the documents in the summaries, they describe the document title, date, and sources quite accurately.

State CDF

Central Decimal File: records of the Department of State in National Archives Record Group 59, General Records of the Department of State.

T 120

Microfilm Publication T 120: records of the German foreign office received from the Department of State in Record Group 242, National Archives Collection of Foreign Records Seized, 1941– . The following citation system is used for National Archives

Microfilm Publications: The Microfilm Publication number followed by a slash, the roll number followed by a slash, and the frame number(s). For example, Document 1 in Volume I: T 120/4638/K325518— K325538.

T 175

Microfilm Publication T 175: records of the Reich leader of the SS and of the chief of the German police in Record Group 242.

U.S. Army and U.S. Air Force

Records relating to the attempts to cause the U.S. Army Air Force to bomb the extermination facilities at Auschwitz and the railroad center at Kaschau leading to Auschwitz, which are part of a variety of records groups and collections in the National Archives. Included are records of the United States Strategic Bombing Survey (Record Group 243), records of the War Refugee Board (Record Group 220), records of the Joint Chiefs of Staff, and other Army record collections.

War Refugee Board

Records of the War Refugee Board, located at the Franklin D. Roosevelt Library in Hyde Park, New York. They are part of National Archives Record Group 220, Records of Temporary Committees, Commissions and Boards. Included in this category are the papers of Myron C. Taylor and Ira Hirschmann.

CONTENTS

Notes

1. *Document 1.* Franz Rademacher was an official in Department Inland II of the German foreign ministry, which provided liaison with the *Reichsleiter* of the SS, Heinrich Himmler, and subordinate SS agencies. Ernst Woermann held various positions in the German foreign ministry, including chief of the political division. A United States military tribunal sentenced him to seven years imprisonment in the "ministries case" at Nuernberg. Deputy Under Secretary Martin Luther of the German foreign ministry was chief of Department Deutschland, which provided the ministry with liaison to the SS. *Obergruppenfuehrer* Reinhardt Heydrich was the dreaded chief of the security police and the security service of the SS. He was assassinated in Prague in 1942. Ernst Bielfeld was an official in the political section of the German foreign ministry.

2. *Document 2.* SS *Hauptsturmfuehrer* Dieter Wisliceny worked in Amt IV of the SS Security Main Office as a subordinate of Adolf Eichmann. He was tried and executed in Czechoslovakia in 1948 for his activities, including deportations of Jews. Curiously enough under interrogation he stated that he worked in Amt IV A 4 in the SS Reich Security Main Office. Eichmann's office was at one time known as IV A 4, whereas later and generally it was IV B 4,

"Evacuations and Jews." Some of the individuals mentioned in the interrogation transcripts are:

- SS *Hauptsturmfuehrer* (Captain) Brunner, a member of Eichmann's Amt IV B 4 whose activities included the deportation of Austrian, particularly Viennese, Jews.
- SS *Obergruppenfuehrer* (Lieutenant General) Ernst Kaltenbrunner, the successor of Reinhardt Heydrich as chief of the security police and the security service. He was sentenced to death by the International Military Tribunal at Nuernberg and executed in October 1946.
- Rudolf Kastner, who held many positions in Jewish organizations in Rumania and Hungary. In the closing years of World War II he worked with the relief committee of the Jewish agency and acted as the vice president of the Assistance and Rescue Committee in Budapest.
- Manfred von Killinger, the German minister in Budapest.
- Hans Elard Ludin, the German ambassador to Slovakia. A court in Czechoslovakia sentenced him to death in 1946.
- SS *Obergruppenfuehrer* Heinrich Mueller, the dreaded chief of Amt IV, Gestapo. After the conclusion of World War II he disappeared, and his whereabouts now are unknown.
- Julius Streicher, the *Gauleiter* of Franconia and the publisher of *Der Stürmer*. The International Military Tribunal at Nuernberg sentenced him to death, and he was executed in October 1946.

3. *Document 3.* The following SS officers belonged to the staff of Adolf Eichmann in Amt IV B 4 of the Reich security main office: Rolf Günther, Otto Hunsche, Theodor Dannecker, Hermann Krumey, and Franz Novak. Richard Gluecks directed the concentration camps upon Eicke's assignment to active duty. Oswald Pohl directed the Economic and Administrative Main Office (WVHA), which controlled the concentration camps. At Nuernberg he was tried in Case 4 by a United States military tribunal and sentenced to death. He was executed in June 1951.

4. *Document 8.* Edmund Veesenmayer was the German minister to and Reich plenipotentiary in Hungary. A United States military tribunal sentenced him in the ministries case to twenty years imprisonment. Otto Winkelmann was the higher SS and police leader in Hungary. SS *Obergruppenfuehrer* Hans Juettner held several leading positions in the Waffen SS. Saly Mayer was the Swiss representative of the American Jewish Joint Distribution Committee.

5. *Document 11.* Lutz Schwerin von Krosigk was German finance minister. A United States military tribunal sentenced him in the ministries case to ten years imprisonment.

6. *Document 13.* SS *Gruppenfuehrer* Odilo Globocnik, who compiled this report, was the higher SS and police leader in the Lublin area. He directed the *Einsatz Reinhardt* killing and plunder actions. In 1945 he committed suicide.

7. *Document 15.* Hans Hohberg was chief of Staff W of the WVHA, which dealt with SS economic enterprises. At Nuernberg he was tried in Case 4 and sentenced to ten years imprisonment by a United States military tribunal.

OFFICE OF CHIEF OF COUNSEL
FOR WAR CRIMES
APO 696 - A   US ARMY

STAFF EVIDENCE ANALYSIS, MINISTRIES DIVISION

By: Betty D. Richardson
Date: 28 October 1947

Document number: NG - 3933

Title and/or general nature: Correspondence between RADEMACH
WOERMANN, and BIELFELD with
regard to HITLER's decision to
abandon the Madagascar project
and send Jews to the East.

Form of Document: A) Carbon copy
B) Original typescript
C) Original typescript

Stamps and other endosements: A) Secret Stamp of D III. Note
in blue pencil - "ab 12/2"
and initials.
B) None.
C) Stamp Secret. Initialled
RADEMACHER. Note in purple
pencil by LUTHER - "Anfrage
habe ich persoenlich beantworte
z.d.a."

Date: A) 10 February 1942
B) 14 February 1942
C) 24 February 1942

Source: D III 1942 Bd. 1
1 - 451 Inl. IIg   4/1 D 519848
now at: Mc Nair Barracks, Berli
FC-SD Mission, Bldg. E.
OCC BET 4840 - A-C

Doc. 1

1

PERSONS OR ORGANIZATIONS IMPLICATED:
RADEMACHER
LUTHER
WOERMANN
BIELFELD
SCHMIEDEN

TO BE FILED UNDER THESE REFERENCE HEADINGS:
NG - Foreign Office
NG - Racial and Political
Persecution.

SUMMARY:
A) RADEMACHER, writing to BIELFELD of Pol X with copy
to SCHMIEDEN, refers to his plan to settle Europe's Jews in
Madagascar, and says HEYDRICH was given orders to put the plan
into effect. Since then, however, the war with Russia has made
other territory available for the final solution", and HITLER
has decided they should be sent East.
B) Note from WOERMANN to RADEMACHER, noting HITLER's
decision to send the Jews to the East, of which BIELFELD has
informed him, and asking where the information comes from.
C) Note from RADEMACHER to LUTHER requesting him to
inform WOERMANN of the talk with HEYDRICH on this matter.

(Analyst's note: See ST. NG - 2586)

END

Councillor of Legation RADEMACHER

SECRET (Stamp)
Berlin, 10 February 1942

Stamp: Foreign Office
        D III 145 secret
        rec'd 12 Feb. 1942
        Encl. (copies) duplicate
        Date received:

Dear Geheimrat!

       In August 1940 I gave you for your files the plan for the final solution of the Jewish Problem, drafted by my office, for which purpose the Madagaskar Island was to be demanded from France in the Peace Treaty, whereas the Reich Security Main Office was to be charged with the actual execution of the task. In accordance with the plan, Gruppen- fuehrer HEYDRICH has been ordered by the Fuehrer to carry out the solution of the Jewish Problem in Europe.

       In the meantime the war against the Soviet Union has offered the possibility to put other territories at our disposal for the final solution. The Fuehrer accordingly decided that the Jews shall not be deported to Madagaskar but to the East. There are it is no longer necessary that Madagaskar be taken into consideration for the final solution.

                                        Heil Hitler !
                                        Yours

                                   signed: RADEMACHER

Transmitted 12 Feb. initial

1.) Minister BIELFELD
     Pol X

Transmitted 12 Feb initial

2.) Senior Councillor of Legation
     von SCHMIEDEN
     Dept. Pol.
                          D III
3.) D III 1451, 1st elaboration is to be deleted and transmitted to
     Minister BIELFELD.

4.) D III 1451, 2nd elaboration will remain with document D III.

5.) for file.

            R 11/Feb

Berlin, 14 February 1942. Re: Pol. X 7 g

Minister BIELFELD informed me of your communication -
D III 145/42 secret - , dated 10 February, according to which the
Fuehrer decided, that the Jews will not be deported to Madagaskar,
but to the East. Therefore it is no longer necessary that
Madagaskar be taken into consideration for the final solution.

In view of the importance of the decision would you
please inform me from which sources the statement derives.

3

Herewith

to Councillor of Legation RADEMACHER

signature: WOERMANN

Branch D III

Re: D III 145/42 secret
         (re: Pol X 7 secret)

SECRET (Stamp)

handwritten notation; across the page
        D III

        Replied personally to inquiry.

        For File

        Initial 26 Feb

        Second initial and date

Note

        The enclosed note refers to the fact that the Madagaskar
plan of Branch D III has become void, due to the new development
as described to Under State Secretary LUTHER by Obergruppenfuehrer HEYDRICH.

Herewith
submitted to Under State Secretary LUTHER

        with the request to inform Under State Secretary WOERMANN
of the conference with Obergruppenfuehrer HEYDRICH.

Berlin, 24 February 1941

                                signature: RADEMACHER

- - - - - - - - - - - - - - -
CERTIFICATE OF TRANSLATION
- - - - - - - - - - - - - - -

                                        28 January 1948

        I, Paul E. GROPP, Civ. No. B 397975, hereby certify that
I am a duly appointed translator for the German and English
languages and that the above is a true and correct translation
of the document NG - 3933

                        Paul E. GROPP
                        Civ. No. B 397975

E R R A T A _ S H E E T

The following corrections should be made:

Page 3, line 9,

    reads: "Initial 26 February"
should read: "(Initial) Luther 26 February"

Page 3, bottom of page,

    add   "(Initial) Rademacher"

5

C E R T I F I C A T E _ O F _ T R A N S L A T I O N

I, Werner Meyer, Civ. B 217471, hereby certify that I am
thoroughly conversant with the German and English languages
and that the above are true corrections of Document No.
NG-3935.

                  Werner Meyer
                  Civ. B 217471

Testimony of Dieter Wisliceny, taken
at Nurnberg, Germany, 14 November 1945,
1430 hours to 1630 hours, by Lt. Col.
Smith W. Brookhart, Jr., OUSCC.

Also present: Lawrence Ecker, Interpreter,
Frances Karr, Court Reporter.

QUESTIONS BY COLONEL BROOKHART TO THE INTERPRETER:

(The interpreter was first duly sworn.)

Q   Will you give your full name, address and duty here?

A   Lawrence Ecker.   I was engaged as an interpreter for
German and English and Russian, if needed.

Q   With the OCC?

A   Yes.

(The witness was duly sworn.)

Doc. 2

6

QUESTIONS BY COLONEL BROOKHART TO THE WITNESS THROUGH THE
INTERPRETER:

Q   What is your name?

A   Dieter Wisliceny.

Q   Where were you born and how old are you?

A   I am 34 years old.   I was born in East Prussia in Regulow-
ken.

Q   Are you married?

A   No.

Q   Are you a member of the Party?

A   Yes.

Q   Since when?

A   Since 1933.

Q   Where did you join?

A   In Silesia.

-1-

Q   What has been your education?

A   I attended the Oberrealschule and graduated.

(The Interpreter: Which is what one might call
a trade high school.)

Q   What has been your length of service in the SS?

A   Since 1934.

Q   What ranks and positions have you held in the SS?

A   I was Hauptsturmfuehrer.

Q   What did you start off as, and when were you made
Hauptsturmfuehrer?

A   I began as an ordinary SS man. I became Hauptsturmfuehrer in 1940.

Q   And where have you had your service; what areas,
countries, camps?

A   I served first in Germany and later abroad.

Q   What years?

A   From 1934 to '37 in Berlin; from '37 to '40 in Danzig;
in Slovakia from '40, and I continued to serve there until the
fall of last year. Then, from February 1943 to December '43
I was in Greece and in Hungary from March 1944 to September '44.

I was detailed from 1940 on to the German Embassy in
Bratislava but during this time I received missions to Greece
and Hungary.

Q   And since September of 1944 what was your service?

A   Since that time I belonged to the RSHA. Since the fall
of last year I had been serving in the RSHA in Berlin.

Q   In what capacity, in this last service?

A I belonged to the Referat of Obersturmbannfuehrer Eichmann.

Q In Amt IV?

A IV A 4.

Q What did you do for Eichmann?

A I belonged to this Referat since 1940, that is, I served in this Referat since 1940.

Q All the time that you were in Czechoslovakia, Greece and Hungary, you were attached to or connected with Eichmann's Referat?

A Yes.

Q What was your prime mission? With what subject did you deal?

A May I explain it in more detail?

Q Yes.

A I have known Eichmann since 1934. We joined the SD together. We worked together in the same Referat from 1934 to 1937. I was, for a time, Eichmann's chief. That was in 1937. I had myself transferred to Danzig in 1937. Until 1940 I had only a loose contact with Eichmann. I saw him only occasionally. In 1938 Eichmann was transferred to Vienna. He directed, in Vienna, the Central Office for Jewish Emigration.

In 1940 I again met Eichmann in Berlin, by accident. He asked me whether I would like to come back to the Referat. He had, in the meantime, become head of it. I said to him, thereupon, that I no longer wished to work in the Central

Office in Berlin. Thereupon he said he needed me for a special job with the Slovak government in Bratislava. I told him, thereupon, if it was a question of a mission abroad, I was at his disposal. For several months I heard nothing more about this matter.

One day, I received the order to report to Berlin, to Eichmann, who would give me further instructions. I then reported to Eichmann in Berlin and he gave me the following explanation:

The Slovak government requested, in a conference with Hitler in Salzburg, that they should obtain German advisors in special fields of economic life and administration, police and so forth. They especially asked for an advisor in the field of the Jewish question. Eichmann had selected me for this post because he believed that I had the necessary qualifications and the proper attitude for an assignment to the Slovak government.

Q Had you any prior service in Czechoslovakia?

A No.

Q Can you speak the language?

A No, I knew no Czechoslovakian, but everybody spoke German well.

I told Eichmann at that time that I was not informed on the way the Jewish problem was being handled in Berlin and asked for exact instructions and directives. I stayed in Berlin for fifteen days to get information, for instructions, and had an opportunity to get an insight into all the files.

Q What was the period of these fifteen days?

-4-

A   This was in August, 1940.

Q   Who instructed when files were made available?

A   Eichmann was, at that time, on leave. I received
instructions from his assistant, Sturmbannfuehrer Rolf
Guenther.

Q   What was Guenther's position?

A   He was Eichmann's personal representative.

Q   In Amt IV A 4?

A   In IV A 4.

Q   What kind of instructions did you receive?

A   I received the following instructions: To advise
the Slovak government on all questions relating to the Jewish problem. To strive, in so far as possible, to see to
it that the Slovak Jewish legislation should be
assimilated, in so far as possible, to the German. This was
the central point or nucleus of the instructions. Everything else was left to me personally. I was to establish
the best possible contact with all Slovak agencies involved.
It was essentially rather a diplomatic than an executive
mission.

I belonged to the German Legation in Bratislava. There
were a certain number of other gentlemen who had similar
missions there.

Q   From the RSHA?

A   In addition to me there was a Criminality Attache,
Franz Holz, Oberregierungsrat Dr. Ludwig Hahn. He was in
charge of the internal administration. From the uniformed

-5-

police there was Captain Kurt Guedler. The latter was intended as an advisor for the Slovakian gendarmerie.

Q What, if any, authority did the Foreign Office have over your mission to Slovakia?

A I was under the Minister. His name was von Killinger. Later the Minister was Ludin. In the legation there was a special section under which all these advisors were. His name was Hans Albrecht Grueninger. We were under this section and we rendered a monthly report on our activity. In all questions that were of any importance, we had to consult with the Minister. The Minister, in every single case, would say how we should proceed. At the Embassy we were in the capacity of Referenten. We belonged to the diplomatic corps and had diplomatic passes.

11

Q Were you a member of the SD throughout this period?

A Yes. I also received my pay from the SD, not from the Foreign Office.

Q Then, your service with the SD has been continuous since 1934?

A Yes, since 1934.

Q During this period, from 1940, until you left the Bratislava Legation, to whom did you make reports in your capacity as SD agent?

A I was used only for this special mission.

Q Did you also report to the Foreign Office or to the local minister?

A Every month I made a report on our activities
in our field of action. I made no report directly to the
Foreign Office, but only to the Minister, and I sent a copy
of my monthly report to Eichmann, that is, the report that I was
made out for the Minister.

Q Did you send anyone else other than Eichmann a copy
of the reports that you sent to Amt IV A 4?

A Four copies always went to Amt IV A 4.

Q But not through the Minister or any other agency?

A No, copies of this report went to Amt IV A 4. But
the Minister knew that these reports were sent to this office.
Copies of them were sent only to IV A 4.

Q Didn't the Minister know that you, as an SD agent,
were not required to keep him advised as to what you reported
to Eichmann?

A Yes. He knew that I rendered these reports and that it
was my duty to render them to the office from which I
received my pay.

Q Who paid you as an SD agent, the State or the Party?

A As an employee of the SD, we were never certain
whether we were being paid by the State or by the Party.
Originally, we were paid only by the Party, but toward the
end, I believe, we were paid by the State.

Q When you were given this fifteen-day course of
instruction in Berlin, what were the basic policies with
regard to Jews that were to be followed by you?

A At that time, in August 1940, the main idea was to
solve the Jewish problem by emigration of the Jews from the

countries occupied by Germany. The intention was, at that time, to force France to open Madagascar for Jewish emigration. The idea was to have emigration to Madagascar from all the countries occupied or controlled by Germany.

Q When was that suggested plan first made known to you?

A August, 1940.

Q That was while you were in Berlin?

A While I was in Berlin. I myself read the memorandums on the subject.

Q Where did the idea originate?

A It originated in Eichmann's Referat.

Q What do you know about Streicher's participation or origination of this idea? He was Gauleiter for Nurnberg.

A He made no contribution to this plan, in all certainty, no.

Q What do you know about Streicher writing articles for publications with this suggestion?

A It was an old plan that had been revived and was very much alive at that time, even among the Jews themselves. I recall that the Zionist leader, Theodore Herzel, had at one time made this proposal when Palestine was closed to the Jews. This plan is not new; it only came up again after the victory over France.

Q And, as you took up your work in Slovakia, how did the policy or plans regarding the Jews change?

A Until the Fall of 1941 this plan had not been definitively discarded. Not until after the beginning of the

13

-8-

war with Russia did any change take place in this respect. From this time on, the plan was dropped; that is, in the Fall of 1941.

Q What took its place?

A At this time Eichmann began to work out a plan whereby all Jews should be deported into Poland and in general, toward the East. At that time he spoke of creating a special reservation in which Jews should be concentrated. In these reservations, they were to be used for particular kinds of work, including armament work, that is, work in the armament industry.

Q Were these reservations in the form of concentration camps?

A There were both kinds, concentration camps or labor camps and also simply ghettos. I saw one of them myself in Sosnowitz, in Upper Silesia.

Q Which kind did you see?

A It was a large dwelling area in Benczin, near Sosnowitz There were about 100,000 Jews living there. The Jews had been concentrated here from all Upper Silesia into this area. The Benczin-Sosnowitz cities are twin cities. Within this dwelling area there were large factories, principally textile factories and furniture factories. The work done there consisted mainly in the manufacture of uniforms and the manufacture of furniture for barracks.

This dwelling area was not closed, like a concentration camp. The Jews were allowed to move around freely in it but were not allowed to leave the reservation.

Q   When was your visit?

A   September, 1941. I was, at that time, with the Slovak Commission in Benczin. The official whom I accompanied at that time was Ministerialrat Dr. Koso, Presidential Chief of the Chancellory. Dr. Koso, as I say, was the Chief of the Presidential Chancellory of Slovakia.

Shall I continue to describe the life in this dwelling area?

Q   First, tell me how long you were in Poland and whether you visited any other Jewish concentration or ghetto districts.

A   I was never in Poland, only in Upper Silesia.

Q   Did you visit any other of the concentration areas for Jews?

A   I was once at a labor camp near Auschwitz -- not Auschwitz -- but a camp that belonged to that area.

Q   On that same trip?

A   No, that was later. I will return later to explain what brought me to this other place.

Q   Tell us about this camp near Sosnowitz, which you visited in September, 1941.

A   All of the places of work of these Jews were under the direction of the Regierungschef of Oppeln, and responsible for carrying out all of the work was the communal supervisor. I do not remember what his name was.

The orders were given to this communal supervisor for the manufacture of so many thousand uniforms and so many

thousand tables or other furniture. The communal supervisor was a Jew and he distributed his work to the different
factories. The materials were delivered and the finished
work was taken away by a German commission, and for the
work performed, food and other daily needs were distributed
among the Jews, and the Jewish communal supervisor distributed
this food and other articles at his own discretion. In this
way it was possible to feed those persons who could no longer
work.

Q   What class of persons are you referring to?

A   Old people, children, women and so on.

Q   What disciplinary controls were used?

A   The communal supervisor himself had police power in
this area, and his own health office.

Q   What was the next higher authority above him?

A   The next highest authority was the Reichsleiter
Regierungschef of Oppeln.

I should like to remark further that the conditions in
this a dwelling area were at that time -- that is in 1941 --
not especially favorable but endurable. This is entirely
objective.

The Slovakian commission, which I accompanied, had an
opportunity to investigate the conditions. We went there
for the following reasons:

The Slovaks intended to establish a number of such work
areas in Slovakia because, as a result of the elimination of
the Jews from business life, some thousands of Jews who had

theretofore been occupied in business, had become un-
employed and the Slovaks requested to be permitted to examine
one of the dwelling areas to get an idea as to whether it
would be worthwhile to establish similar dwelling areas
in Slovakia.

This trip was not especially prepared, but really,
just improvised. We went to Sosnowitz because it was closest
to Slovakia, and could be reached by automobile.

Q What did you decide after you visited it?

A The Slovak government thereupon established in
Sered and in Novaky two such work centres. In Sered a
large furniture factory and in Novaky a number of textile
mills were established. About 4,000 Jews were occupied in
those together. These work centres continued to exist
until the Slovak uprising in September, 1944. The Jews
in these two work centres were relatively free; they had
their own administration. The Slovak state was the only
placer of orders for these two work centres. The two work
centres were an excellent business for the Slovak government
financially. The two manufacturing centres are not to be
compared with concentration camps. They were lodged in old
stone barracks.

Q What was the death rate in these Jewish communities
in Slovakia?

A The mortality was quite normal. The Jews at these
places were completely free except that they could not leave
that reservation.

Q What happened after the uprising of September, 1944?

A A part of the people, who were in these work centres, joined the rebels. The rebellion was made by the Slovak army, and it took place in this area where the two work centres were. I was no longer there, but when the uprising had been quelled, the Jews were captured, were taken to Sered and from there to Auschwitz.

Q All of them?

A Not only the Jews in these two places, but all the Jews in general who were still in Slovakia, were concentrated at this place and sent from there to Auschwitz.

Q What did you have to do with that?

A I was, at that time, in Hungary, on a mission from Eichmann.

Q Who had been in charge of collecting all the Slovakian Jews and sending them to Auschwitz?

A Hauptsturmfuehrer Brunner.

Q What did Eichmann have to do with this collection and shipment?

A He ordered it.

Q What did Kaltenbrunner have to do with it?

A He was Eichmann's chief. All the moves that Eichmann made had to be approved by Kaltenbrunner.

Q Do you know that of your own knowledge?

A I know that positively.

Q Why are you so positive?

A May I explain the formal manner in which this was done?

Q In detail, please.

A Eichmann's office was Amt IV A 4. That belonged to the
office of Amt IV. And the chief of that office was Mueller.
He was General of the Police and SS Gruppenfuehrer.

Q Obergruppenfuehrer?

A No, Gruppenfuehrer.

Mueller was directly under Kaltenbrunner. All measures that
were taken in the field of the Jewish problem were submitted for
fundamental decisions to Kaltenbrunner; first Heydrich and later
Kaltenbrunner, that is after the death of Heydrich.

Q Do you know it to be a fact that the same situation prevailed under Kaltenbrunner as had prevailed under Heydrich on
Jewish questions?

A No change occurred after Heydrich's death in the treatment
of the Jewish problem, of that I am positive. The measures were
taken against the Jews in 1942, and continued to be handled in
the same way after Kaltenbrunner became chief.

I saw, with my own eyes, in the Referat in Berlin, drafts
that were being directed to Himmler, but all these reports and
decisions always went through Kaltenbrunner. It was an entirely
clear responsibility. Eichmann could do nothing without the
approval of Mueller and, in very special cases, the approval of
Kaltenbrunner.

Further, I should like to add that Eichmann and Kaltenbrunner
knew each other very well. They were both from Linz and Eichmann was in special favor with Kaltenbrunner.

Q How do you know that?

A From Eichmann himself.

Q What did he tell you?

A Kaltenbrunner was formerly an attorney in Linz. He knew Eichmann's family very well, and they knew each other since the time when they were both illegal Nazis in Austria, and they also knew each other from the time when they were both in Vienna in 1938; that is when both were in Vienna. Eichmann told me personally that whenever he had any special diffi- culties he appealed at once to Kaltenbrunner.

Q Kaltenbrunner said he did not know Eichmann very well. What do you say about that?

A He knew him very well.

I have known Eichmann since 1934. When Kaltenbrunner was made Chief of the Security Police and Eichmann said, at that time, that he had especially good connections with Kalten- brunner.

Q And that especially good connection continued through the years?

A Yes, until February of this year, definitely.

Q Why did it end then?

A I do not know whether it ended at that time. In February, 1945, I saw Eichmann for the last time, and at that time the good relations still existed.

Q What happened to Eichmann after that?

A I know positively he was in Theresienstadt am in April, 1945, because I telephoned him there and they said he had just left. At that time, Count Bernadotte, head of the International Red Cross, was visiting the Theresienstadt. I

was to conduct Count Bernadotte, on this occasion, on his
visit to Theresienstadt. But I did not go to Theresienstadt.
I called Eichmann at that time and wanted to see him, but he
had already left Theresienstadt. I spoke to Eichmann the last
time in February and he said, "If things go wrong, I will go
to Prague and will shoot my wife, my children and myself."

Since that time I have heard nothing more from him, either
from him or about him.

Q Why did you understand Eichmann intended to kill himself
and his family?

A He himself told me in February "If things go wrong, I
will go to Prague and shoot my wife, my children, and myself."

Q Why did he consider it necessary to kill himself and
his family?

A That is quite explainable; because he realized that he
bore the main responsibility for the death of five million
people.

Q How did he arrive at that figure?

A I know this rather exactly by way of calculations.

Q Tell us the basis of your exact calculations.

A We established this calculation with Dr. Kastner.

Q What do you mean by "We"?

A Dr. Kastner and I had made this computation. Dr. Kastner was the delegate of the Joint Distribution Committee.
We made this calculation last fall in Hungary.

Q What was the occasion?

A As far as I recall, Dr. Kastner was gathering material
for a comprehensive report to be submitted to Roosevelt. Mr.

McCleland, a deputy of President Roosevelt for Refugees, was
in Switzerland. Dr. Kastner called him. The figure consisted
of the number of Jews in Poland, about one-half millionpersons,
and of one-half million Jews from Hungary, Jews from France,
Belgium and Holland, from Slovakia, Greece, Denmark, Germany,
Bohemia and Moravia. Not included in this number are the Jews
from the Russian territory.

We -- that is, Dr. Kastner and I -- discussed these figures
at the time and so far as I was able, I checked up the figures.

Q What other figures can you give by countries?

A I do not have them all in my head, but some of them I
still know: 50,000 for Slovakia, Greece 55,000, Hungary
460,000.

Q You already gave 500,000.

A Almost 500,000, but the exact figure is 460,000. There
were undoubtedly 500,000, but 40,000 did not go to Auschwitz
but other camps. As to France, Holland and Belgium, I would
have to go over those figures. Maybe in the next hearing I
can submit the figures.

Q Do you have any other figures now?

A If I may think over the matter somewhat first. I must
put together things that lie apart in time and space.

Q Does this figure of 5,000,000 represent your estimate
of the number of persons killed?

A Could we put it this way: That these figures represent
the number of people who were sent to places where it was
intended to exterminate them. I do not know how many of these

persons may have escaped extermination as a result of liberation through the advance of the Russian and other armies.

Q Why do you attribute all the deaths to Eichmann?

A He was that man in the RSHA who was responsible for all these measures. I myself, in the summer of 1942, had an opportunity to see a letter from Himmler to the Chief of the Security Police, in which Himmler ordered the so-called final solution of the Jewish problem. Responsible for this was the Chief of the Security Police, that is responsible for the execution of this order, in conjunction with the Inspector of the Concentration Camp System. In this letter it was expressly emphasized that this decision was being taken at Hitler's order.

Q What was the solution on the Jewish problem, as contained in this letter?

23

A Complete biological extermination of the Jews. The only restriction or limitation was that Jews capable of work should be used in concentration camps for armament manufacture. Eichmann decided that a certain number of thousands of Jews should be sent to Auschwitz. In Auschwitz those Jews who were able-bodied, who could work in these plants, were sorted out and the rest were exterminated. In this sense the Inspector of the Concentration Camp System and the Chief of Security Police were jointly responsible for the carrying out of this program.

Q Who did the sorting and made the determination of those to be executed?

A All were sent to Auschwitz or Lublin. I do not know who did the actual sorting, but it was some physician or other.

-18-

I assume it was a physician, that is, I assume that the actual sorting was done by some physician.

Q When you say that the administration for Concentration Camps in RSHA were jointly responsible, whom do you mean?

A Eichmann was commissioned by Kaltenbrunner in the RSHA. In the VWHA it was Brigade Leader Glicks. I believe he writes it with an "i", but I am not absolutely sure.

Q Who else?

A Responsible for Auschwitz was Hauptobersturmfuehrer Hoess. I often saw this Hoess at Eichmann's. For Lublin it was Globotschnig. He was in the SS and Police Commander in Lublin. The notorious Maidanek Camp was under Globotschnig.

Q What did Pohl have to do in the Concentration Camp set-up?

A Pohl was the head of the whole Concentration Camp System. Glicks was under him. It was the same relationship as between Eichmann and Kaltenbrunner.

COLONEL BROOKHART: That will be all for now.

APPROVED _____
Interrogator

_____
Interpreter

_____
Court Reporter

Testimony of Dieter Wisliceny, taken at
Nurnberg, Germany, on 15 November, 1945,
1435-1740, by Lt. Col. Smith W. Brookhart,
Jr., IGD, OUSCC: And Mr. Sender Jaari.
Also present: Mr. George A. Sakheim,
Interpreter; Thomas Haynes, Court Reporter.

QUESTIONS BY LT. COL. BROOKHART TO THE WITNESS THROUGH THE
INTERPRETER:

Q   You are the same Dieter Wisliceny who appeared
this morning, and you understand you are speaking under oath?

A   Yes.

Q   Referring to your statement of this morning, as to
the number of Jews estimated to have been affected by actions
of the RSHA since 1941, what are you able to say as to the
number in each of the designated areas who died or were
executed or disappeared?

A   Since 1942, by order of Himmler, Jews were only valued
as workers. All other Jews, who were not used in that capacity,
were to be executed by order of Himmler.

Q   Do you mean all those others than the able-bodied
were to be executed?

A   I mean by that specifically women, women with
children, old people, and those who had an afflication of some
kind.

Q   Were all to be executed?

A   Yes. At one time, Eichmann told me that the
percentage of Jews who did (this) work, amounted to something like
from 20 to 25%

Q   Did you say 20 or 25% were able to work, or 20 to
25% were unable to work?

A   Were able to work.

Q   Did the 25% considered able to work include any women or children?

A   Yes, in those 20 to 25% women and children were included that were considered fit to live.

Q   For the children, what age was chosen to determine whether they were of value and therefore fit to live?

A   I can't say it exactly but I believe from 12 to 13 years upward.

Q   Who made the determination as to the fitness of the Jews to survive?

A   That came from the inspector of concentration camps. The whole question of the annihilation of the Jews was brought about in closed camps.

Q   You are speaking now of the camps that were closed, as distinguished from those labor and factory areas that you described yesterday?

A   Yes. I came to know about a number of such extermination camps.

Q   Their names?

A   The largest one was Auschwitz, Maidenek, near Lublin. In the immediate vicinity of Lublin there were several other such camps.

Q   Do you remember their names?

A   No, because the designations for these transports always went by the name of Lublin. Maidenek too, was never mentioned by name, but was always referred to in the record

Wisliceny

by Camp M. It was only by accident that I learned one time that this Camp M was Maidenek.

Q   How did that come about?

A   When the Russians took over the camp at Maidenek, with all of its devices, Eichmann once mentioned that this camp, Maidenek, was our Camp M.

Q   He said that to you in a conversation?

A   Yes.

Q   What designation did Auschitz have?

A   Auschwitz was commonly known as Camp A.

Q   What was Camp T?

A   If I correctly recollet, that belonged to the complex Lublin system. I remember having heard the designation Camp T.

Q   Was that also an annihilation camp?

A   Yes, sir.

Q   Were there others?

A   As far as I can remember now, there were none. Later on, when everything was concentrated in Auschwitz, certainly in the period 1943 - 1944.

Q   How do you classify camps Mauthausen, Dachau and Buchenwald?

A   They were normal concentration camps from the point of view of the department of Eichmann.

Q   When you referred to Auschwitz and the several camps at Lublin as being annihilation camps, were you speaking primarily from the standpoint of the annihilation of the Jews?

A   Only the extermination of the Jews. About other

-3-   Wisliceny

things I can't say anything as I don't know anything exactly.

Q   When in 1942 did Himmler issue the order that you have already described?

A   It must have been in the spring of 1942. May I say how I got to know about this order?

Q   Anything you know.

A   In the spring of 1942 I received the assignment from Eichmann to demand of the Slovak Government, the furnishing of between 15,000 to 20,000 single Jews for labor purposes. These Jews were supposed to work in the armament industry. This contingent of 15,000 to 20,000 Jews was supposed to be accredited to the Slovak Government on its regular quota of workers which they were supposed to furnish. The Slovak government had offered, of its own accord, to furnish Jewish workers for the German armament industry. This proposal was then accepted, and I received the assignment to request 15,000 to 20, 000 Jewish workers from the Minister of the Interior. That took place in March or April of the year 1942. These labor forces — were transported by rail, and their destination was Auschwitz and Lublin. Auschwitz was at that time in the process of construction. This labor contingent was not exterminated but was actually used for labor purposes. In May 1942 the Slovak Government asked whether the families of these workers could not be transferred to the Reich, because they were depending on the support of the Slovak state, as their providers were in Germany. No arrangements had been made for the transfer of funds back to

-4-   Wisliceny

Slovakia, for the maintenance of dependents there. At that time Eichmann was in Bratislavia. He visited Minister Mach and the Prime Minister Tuka, accompanied by me. During this visit, this question was discussed. Eichmann declared himself prepared to accept these families into the Reich area, specifically into Poland. He gave Minister Mach and Prime Minister Tuka the assurance that these Jewish families would be assembled in the area in Lublin in the towns and villages which had been evacuated by the Polish civilian population. He gave the same assurance to Ambassador Ludin, and he left even me in doubt as to what disposition was going to be made of the families.

I want to add to this that this was made so much easier because during my work in Bratislavia, I only came to Berlin very seldom at that time. The first contingent of workers -- that is the single men -- were 17,000 and the families which were there in May and June 1942 amounted to 32,000 to 33,000 people. They were sent by the Slovak government. Then a pause took place between the transports.

In July, Prime Minister Tuka summoned me to him and asked for an explanation as to what had happened to the Jewish families in Poland. In particular, he was concerned about the fate about those Jews who had been christened, and he asked for permission that these people would have the right to follow their Christian religion. He also requested that a Slovak commission be permitted to travel in these areas that were occupied by Jews in order to ascertain the well-being of these people. This action of a Slovak government was based upon the diplomatic action of the Papal Nuncio, Monseignor Burzio.

29

-5-

The request of Prime Minister Tuka was then given verbally to the German embassy.

The Ambassador then dispatched me to Berlin to talk matters over with Eichmann and requested that the wish of the Slovak government be granted. I then went to Berlin. That was July, 1942, the end of July or the beginning of August 1942. During this time no further transports went from Slovakia into Poland. I then had a very serious talk with Eichmann and also supported this point and told him the wish of the Slovak government should be granted because otherwise our international prestige would suffer very seriously. I referred him to the statement of the Pope and the state secretary, Maglione. They had been made in public and in addition to that, to the Slovak Ambassador in Rome, at the Vatican.

30

I further pointed out that the President, Dr. Tiso, was himself a Catholic priest, and that the Slovak government had only agreed to the deportation of Jews, to Poland, on condition that they would be treated humanely.

Eichmann then stated that a visit by a Slovak commission in the area of Lublin would be impossible. When I asked him why, he said, after much delay and a great deal of discussion, that there was an order of Himmler according to which all Jews were to be exterminated. When I asked him who was going to assume the responsibility for this order, he said that he was prepared to show me this order in writing which had been signed by Himmler. I then requested that he show me this order. This order was under the classification of Top Secret. This discussion took

-6-   (Wisliceny)

place in his study in Berlin. He was sitting at his desk, and I was in the same position, opposite him, as I am now opposite the Colonel. He took this order from his safe. It was a thick file. He then searched and took out this order. It was directed to the Chief of the Security Police and the Security Service.

The contents of this order went something like this. I cannot give it precisely since I am under oath, but it is approximately as follows. The Fuehrer has decided that the final disposition of the Jewish question is to start immediately. By the code word, "final disposition" was meant the biological extermination of the Jews. Himmler had put the limitation on this order that at the present time able bodied Jews who could be used for work were to be excluded.

Q   Did Himmler put that order into the Hitler order, or was it included in the text of the order?

A   "I designate the Chief of the Security Police and Security Service and the Inspector of Concentration Camps with the execution of this order." Excepted from this order were those few in concentration camps who were needed within the framework of the labor program. The particulars of this program were to be agreed upon between the Chief of the SD and the Security Police and the Inspector of Concentration Camps. I am to be informed currently about the execution of this order. I saw with my own eyes the signature of Himmler under this order.

Q   What was the date of the order?

A   I can't say exactly, but it must have been from the end of April or the beginning of May 1942.

-7-   (Wislicency)

Q   Do you know whether it was addressed to Heydrich
or not?

A   Yes, it was addressed to Heydrich.

Q   In other words, it was issued before Heydrich's death?

A   Yes.

Q   Did Eichmann have the original letter?

A   Yes.

Q   You saw the original letter in Eichmann's office?

A   Yes.

Q   Did Eichmann have the original letter?

A   Yes.

Q   You saw the original letter in Eichmann's office?

A   Yes, I saw the original order.

32

Q   It was addressed to whom?

A   It was addressed to the Chief of the Security Service
and the Police. The second title was to the head of the WVHA,
to whom the Inspector of the Concentration camps was subordinated.
It was an official decree, with an official title.

There were also other letters from Himmler to Heydrich
and Kaltenbrunner, which were addressed, "Dear Heydrich" or
"Dear Kaltenbrunner." In this case it was an official decree.
It was surrounded by a red border as a special delivery document.

Q   And immediate action document?

A   Yes, urgent document. I was very much impressed
by this document which gave him so much power to use as he saw
fit, and to which Eichmann gave me explanatory comments. I
believe I said at that time, "May God prevent that our enemies

-8-   (Wisliceny)

should ever do anything similar to the German people."

Q What did Eichmann say?

A That I shouldn't get sentimental, this was a Fuehrer Order. I realized that this meant the death warrant for millions of people, and that now in Eichmann's hands was concentrated the power to execute this order the way he saw fit.

During the further course of the conversation, Eichmann ordered me through delaying action, to try to stall off the request of the Slovak Government for visiting the areas occupied by Jews in the Lublin section.

Q Referring again to the order, who did you understand was to be responsible in the RSHA for the execution of this order?

A Kaltenbrunner and Gruppenfuehrer Mueller.

Q Kaltenbrunner wasn't in office at that time. This is between Heydrich's death and Kaltenbrunner's appointment, if it was in August of 1942.

A Yes, but this action continued. This order was never withdrawn and it continued right on to be effective. He took over this order when he assumed office.

Q Go ahead with what happened when Eichmann talked to you.

A Eichmann gave me the order to put pressure upon the Slovak Government to have the remaining 25,000 to 30,000 Jews also evacuated.

I then returned to Bratislava with the decision not to execute this order, if possible.

At that time there were still several thousand Jews in the collecting camps which have been instituted by the Slovak Government. These Jews were destined for transport. Since I was unable to give the

-9-   (Wisliceny)

33

Slovak Government a positive answer to their request, they delayed the transport of these Jews in the collecting camp.

Undoubtedly, however, these Jews would also have been transported if a hard pressure had been brought to bear upon the Slovak Government by the German Government. I then had a lengthy interview with the German Ambassador, Ludin. Ludin also took the point of view in this question, that he did not want to exert any pressure upon the Slovak Government. The whole question was unpleasant enough for him. This I gathered from several conversations with him. He could never understand the point of view of Himmler in this question.

In August or the beginning of September 1942, the Joint Distribution Committee approached me through an intermediary. This intermediary was a Jew by the name of Karl Hochberg. I had known him for sometime, as he had on some occasions before done some statistical work for me. He worked in the Jewish Central Organization in Slovakia. We had on frequent occasions discussed the Jewish question and problem in a confidential manner. He had questioned me at the time whether there was no possibility that these transports of Jews from Slovakia could be prevented. I told him at that time that if it depended upon me, no further transports of Jews would leave Slovakia, but I did not tell him the real reason that was known to me.

Hochberg told me at the time that if an understanding could be reached between the Jews, as represented by the Joint Distribution Committee, and the German officials

Wislicency

and agencies, any amount of money would be available for that.
I told him that my personal disposition towards this question
did not depend on money or money matters. Hochberg stated
that the man who had given him this assignment was a person
named Rott, of Zurich, Switzerland. I assumed that this
Rott was Nathan Schwalb or Sally Meyer, whose names I learned
later.

Hochberg, on two occasions, showed me post cards from
this Rott. In September Hochberg came to my office and gave
me the amount of twenty thousand American dollars.

Q   What kind of currency?

A   In dollars. To begin with I declined to accept
this money, if it were intended for me personally. At that
time I earned so much money that I did not want to have
my point of view bought or to be obligated to anybody.

Q   Do you mean you received so much by way of
salary?

A   My income came from three sources: My salary
which I received from SD, per diem, and in addition to that
I received five thousand Slovakian Kronen, the equivalent
of five hundred marks, from the German ambassador for
purposes of representation. At that time I earned more
than twelve hundred marks a month. This income was a very
considerable one because Slovakia was a very cheap country
in which to live.

Q   What did you do about Hochberg's offer of the
twenty thousand dollars?

      Wisliceny

35

A   I said to Hochberg that with the twenty thousand dollars I would make an attempt to influence Eichmann the way Hochberg wanted me to.

As a resumé of my discussions with Hochberg, I wrote a record to Eichmann in which I stated the following: I stated that the Joint Distribution Committee would be prepared to pay any possible sum if an agreement could be reached concerning the fate of the Jews in the territory occupied by Germany.

Q   What reply did you get?

A   I added in this report that a sum up to three million dollars was available for this purpose. That was the sum that Hochberg had mentioned to me. I also added the fact that I had received twenty thousand dollars and declared this sum to the aid for Theresienstadt. I asked for a decision on this report as to what was to be done in the disposition of this money and how I should continue my negotiations with the representative of the Joint Committee.

For a long time after the submission of this report, I didn't hear anything. I know however, that extracts from my record were submitted to Himmler.

Q   How do you know that?

A   Eichmann told me that himself. I subsequently saw the decision which Himmler reached.

Q   In what form did you see it?

A   I was summoned back to Berlin.

Q   When?

-12-   Wisliceny

A   In the beginning of November 1942. I was shown an order from Himmler that was signed by his adjutant, Suchaneck. It stated that the twenty thousand dollars would be delivered immediately and that I should attempt to elicit another large sum from this Jew.

Q   What did you do?

A   If this suceeded, I was to be released from Bratislavia. The twenty thousand dollars was picked up by a special courier in Bratislavia from me.

Q   When?

A   In November 1942, about the same time that I saw this letter.

Q   And then what?

A   I said to Hochberg at the time that the discussions had reached a deadlock and that I did not want to accept any further sums from him; that I could give him the assurance that my personal disposition towards this case, as I have stated in August before I had ever received any amount of money from him, would remain unchanged.

Q   What was done with this money?

A   This money was directed to the WVHA in Berlin.
Eichmann told me at that time in Berlin that I was to drop all further negotiations and that if anything would go wrong, he would have no hesitancy aboutdropping me entirely; that he would not protect me against any action by superiors.

Q   Now, let's move on to the action that followed. We were talking about the Jews that had been moved from Slovakia

-13-   Wisliceny

to Poland. Without quite so much detail what was the disposition of the 17,000, and the 33,000 members of their families?

A   These 17,000, as far as I know, were employed in construction of the camp Auschwitz. I know that because, for the larger part, these people were still writing letters even at the end of two years, so they were alive.

Q   What about their families, the 32,000 or 33,000?

A   These families went to Auschwitz, where they were exterminated. Part of them, however, remained alive and were used in the construction work.

Q   How soon after their shipment from Slovakia to Auschwitz did the executions begin?

A   As far as I know, as soon as the transport from Slovakia reached Auschwitz.

Q   Let's see how your dates check up. You did not see Himmler's execution order until August, is that right?

A   Yes, but the order was issued in April. I only gathered from my conversations with Eichmann that these things were taking place and that these people were no longer alive. He said to me at that time verbally, "The Slovaks won't be able to see their Jews anymore because they are no longer alive."

Q   Which was the group that you say continued to write for two years and therefore must have been alive?

A   The first transport, made up of the 17,000 workers, and also the other transports, those who were left alive in order to be used for work.

Q   Was the same ratio that you have previously
referred to, about 20 to 25 per cent of the total, all that
remained alive out of these groups as able-bodied?

A   The first 17,000 had been selected and were
healthy and fit to work, and as far as I know, they all
remained alive. The ratio that I mentioned before related
to an average of all these figures.

COL. BROOKHART: The witness is pointing to
Exhibit A.

A   This percentage I did not calculate myself.
This ratio I gathered from a conversation between Eichmann
and Obersturmbannfuehrer Hoess, which took place in July in
1944 in Budapest. Obersturmbannfuehrer Hoess, the commandant,
of Auschwitz, said that out of all of the transports from
all of the German occupied Europe, 20 and a maximum of 25
per cent could be used to work.

Q   Did he indicate that from 75 to 80 per cent had
been exterminated at Auschwitz of those who had arrived there?

A   Yes.

Q   Did he give any figure as to how many had been
executed up to that time in July 1944?

A   No, I only heard parts of the conversation. This
conversation concerned itself with the percentage of able-bodied
Jews that could be expected out of the evacuation of Jews
from Hungary. That is why other figures relating to the
Jews that had been exterminated at Auschwitz were not discussed in this conversation.

-15-   Wisliceny

Q   Out of the 500,000 Hungarian Jews that you have put down in your table here, as being the number that you personally knew to have been affected by the RSHA actions, how many went to Auschwitz?

A   460,000.

Q   460,000 out of the estimated 500,000 all went to Auschwitz?

A   Yes, they all went to Auschwitz.

Q   How many of those that went to Auschwitz were killed?

A   That I can't say exactly.

Q   What information do you have?

A   I only know that the percentage mentioned by Hoess referred to this figure.

Q   Do you have any other information from any other source as to what disposition was made of the 450,000 Hungarian Jews at Auschwitz?

A   Only insofar as Eichmann openly declared that out of the 460,000 Jews, all but the 20 per cent before mentioned were exterminated.

Q   Do you know what methods were used to exterminate Jews at Auschwitz?

A   As Eichmann told me in a conversation, they were killed in gas chambers with carbon monoxide gas.

Q   At what date did they first start using gas chambers at Auschwitz?

A   I can't say for sure, but certainly as early

Wisliceny

as 1942.

Q   Did you visit Auschwitz?

A   No, I never visited Auschwitz itself, but a labor camp in the vicinity of Auschwitz where Slovaks were employed.

Q   That is one you referred to earlier today, that visit?

A   Yesterday I mentioned it.

Q   Were all Hungarian Jews sent to Auschwitz?

A   All.

Q   What about the other 40,000 that you have included in your total estimate here in Exhibit A?

A   Part of them, approximately 30,000, were used during October and November, 1944, for the construction of the so-called East Wall, which I mentioned this morning. From about 9,000 to 10,000 Jews were used in the vicinity of Vienna for agricultural laborers in small groups and also in small enterprises. These Jews were still in Vienna when Vienna was taken by the Russians and were under the control of Obersturmbannfuehrer Kurmey, to whose command I belonged.

Q   I didn't quite understand. Were there 10,000 under Kurmey's orders or the whole 40,000?

A   Only the 9,000 to 10,000 Jews were under the control of Kurmey. The other 30,000 were under the control of Gau Leiterung Headquarters, Lower Danube, which control the construction of the South East Wall. Several contingents

41

of the transports of the 50,000 were not used in the construction of the Southeast Wall, but were sent to a concentration camp near Weiden in the Oberpfalz. The 9,000 to
10,000 Jews who were under the command of Kurney were not
in any concentration camps but were almost at complete
liberty in Vienna. These Jews were saved -- to use the term
of Eichmann -- for the purpose of negotiations going on
between Himmler's representatives and those of the Joint
Committee.

Q   Will you prepare a statement projecting the
figures that you have already set down in Exhibit A for the
several countries, indicating the disposition of these Jews,
first as to the concentration camps to which they were sent
or the industry they were assigned, and, insofar as you
have any knowledge or information, the number that were
executed and the number that survived?

A   Yes, with the limitation that it is so far as
it is known to me.

Q   Now, I have asked Mr. Jaari to go over these
exhibits that you have prepared since the preceding session.

(At this point Col. Brookhart left the room, and
the interrogation was conducted by Mr. Jaari.)

Q   Do you need some further information in order
to work out this new estimate?

A   I'd like to have a piece of paper in order to
be able to sketch this briefly. I'll jot down the figures
and copy the plan for the estimate.

-18-   Wisliceny

MR. JAARI: The witness shows two charts he has worked on since the previous session. What does Exhibit B describe?

A   The Colonel requested this morning that I draw up a chart about Eichmann's department showing who was responsible to whom, who gave orders to whom, and how Eichmann fitted into the whole set-up, and the personnel of the department.

Q   And the chart that we'll call Exhibit C?

A   Exhibit C is the department for Slovakia and the protectorate in which I worked for some days in January and February of this year.

Q   Now, Exhibit B, will you explain to me in detail Exhibit B?

A   At the head of the RSHA was Kaltenbrunner, who was directly responsible to Himmler. Next came Department IV, called the Gestapo or Secret Police, headed by Gruppenfuehrer Mueller. This department is subdivided into several groups. These groups are designated with capital letters.

Group A, to which the section of Eichmann belonged, had no head. Section IV A 4 was one of several sections belonging to Group IV A. Section IV A 4 was headed by Obersturmbannfuehrer Eichmann. This section had two subsections. The Section IV A 4/a was the subsection dealing with questions of the church.

-19-   Wisliceny

43

Then the subsection IV A 4 b was the subsection for Jewish questions.

Q   The sections or the offices which belong under subsection IV A 4 b you have shown clearly underneath?

A   Yes.

Q   On the right side of the paper you have written some names.

A   On the right side of the page, I have shown the personnel that belonged directly to the subsection of Eichmann and the functions of this personnel. I would like you to read this and see if you have any questions about it.

Q   This is how the subsection was in the spring of 1944?

A   In the spring. In the spring of 1944 certain changes in personnel took place in Eichmann's subsection.

Q   When did the persons whose names you have listed here -- when were they appointed?

A   Eichmann was appointed in 1940. His deputy, Gunther, and also Hunsche joined the subsection in 1942. As far as the others are concerned, I don't know exactly when they joined the subsection.

Q   The names in the lower right hand corner had functions in different countries?

A   Obersturmbannfuehrer Dannecker, for example, was at different times in France, Italy, Bulgaria and Hungary. With the others listed here, still referring to the lower right hand corner, things were similar. Brunner

Wisliceny

was at different times in Vienna, Salonika, Greece, France
and finally in Slovakia.

Q   Was that Karl Brunner?

A   No, Louis Brunner.

Q   You use the expression "Schweinhund" in
connection with Brunner's name. Why did you do that?

A   He was an extremely unscrupulous individual,
one of the best tools of Eichmann. He never had an opinion of
his own, and as Eichmann himself described him, he was "one
of my best men."

Q   Do you know where he is now?

A   At the end he was in Vienna. The last time I
saw him was the 2nd of April, 1945.

Q   If we have this chart prepared or copied, are
you willing to sign it under oath?

A   Yes.

Q   Now we will talk about Exhibit C.

A   Exhibit C is worked out according to the same
principles as Exhibit B, showing that the line of responsibility
went up directly to Kaltenbrunner. Group IV B dealt with
foreign countries -- partly countries occupied by Germany and
partly countries under German influence. Sub-section IV B 2 c
was under the leadership of Sturmbannfuehrer Schoneseiffen.

Q   Is that the same man you mentioned this
morning?

A   Yes. On the right hand side, the personnel
of the Sub-section is mentioned. I want to point out that,

Wisliceny

45

of course, both upon Exhibit B and C, I have not mentioned the lower employees.

Q   And you are willing to do the same thing with this Exhibit as with Exhibit B?

A   Yes.

Q   Now, coming back to your last statement, on what happened to Slovak Jews, was Slovakia finally cleaned of Jews?

A   No, up UNTIL ~~to~~ the Slovak insurrection it was not. There remained roughly 25,000 Jews; I cannot say the exact number because some of them could not be ascertained statistically. Besides that, quite a high percentage of Jews were still active in the economic life of Slovakia.

Q   You mean the 25,000 were alive and working until the insurrection?

A   Yes.

Q   What happened to them then?

A   After the Slovak insurrection had broken out, I attempted personally to get back to Bratislavia.

Q   When was that?

A   That was in September 1944. At that time I was in Hungary with Eichmann. At that time Eichmann refused the suggestion, because I no longer had his confidence.

Q   Was that the same matter that you described in the morning session?

A   No. This was another matter. He suspected me of having aided the president of the Orthodox Jewish

-22-

Wisliceny

Community, Dr. Philip Freudiger, in escaping with his family from Budapest to Rumania. This was a fact that I aided him, but Eichmann could not prove it. He also suspected me of being in too close personal contact with Dr. Kastner, the delegate of the Joint Committee in Budapest.

Q   But what did you learn of the fate of the 25,000 Jews?

A   Eichmann or rather his deputy, Gunther, sent the SS Capt. Brunner to Slovakia. Brunner had been in Paris until August.

Q   And what measures did Brunner take in Slovakia?

A   Brunner belonged to the command of TSD and the Security Police in Bratislava. The name of this commander was Obersturmbannfuehrer Litiska.

Q   Why does Litiska's name not appear on your chart?

A   He was not under Eichmann. The commanders were directly under the RSHA. Brunner in a large action had arrested all Jews in the territory re-occupied by German troops in Slovakia and had them sent to Camp Sered.

Q   This was when?

A   October, 1944.

Q   The whole action was finished within one month?

A   Yes, because in Bratislava all of the Jews were still present in their dwellings, and there this action took place during one night, and all of the Jews who had fallen into the hands of the German troops or Slovakian police during the reoccupation of the country were delivered to this Camp Sered. They were then sent to Auschwitz in several transports by Brunner, although I, as well as the Stendartenfuehrer Becher, tried to prevent the transport from taking place. Becher at that time was in Budapest, negotiating as Himmler's representative with the representatives of the Joint Distribution Committee.

Q   And in Auschwitz they were exterminated?

A   Yes.

Q   How did you learn about that?

A   In October 1944 I was myself in Bratislava.

Q   Against Eichmann's order?

A   Eichmann knew about it. I gave as the reason for that, that I would have to report to the German Ambassador in order to take leave there, since my mission in Slovakia had been completed. I tried to save Frau Fleischmann, the representative of the Joint Committee in Slovakia, from going along in his transport, but Brunner refused that. He gave as a reason for this refusal that Frau Fleischmann had made atrocity propaganda.

Q   So you did not succeed in saving anyone from this transport?

A   No. Brunner pointed out to me that now he was the expert dealing with these matters and that I was not to interfere with his duties. He was always afraid that I should still return to Slovakia in time and therefore hurried the transports very much.

-24-   Wisliceny

Q   After this time Slovakia was cleaned of Jews?

A   Yes, with the exception of those people that were in hiding or that were hid by Slovaks; there must have been several thousand. For example, one of them was the well-known Rabbi Weissmantel, who was known to me.

Q   In order to take up another matter, you told us this morning that you had read the files on American-British mission in Slovakia; that you read them during the three days you worked at Trebnitz.

A   Yes, sir, What about it?

Q   What did you learn about it?

A   This mission had arrived by plane from Bari and landed in the vicinity of Banska Bystrika, which was the headquarters of the insurrection, and had the task to collect and help Allied fliers, who had forced landings, to treturn to Italy. In addition to that, they were supposed to accept requests for aid and arms of General Viest, the leader of the Slovakian Army and pass them on to the Allies. The leader of the British was a Capt. Sehmer. The leader of the American mission was a man called Brown, I believe. The names of the other members of the mission I cannot remember anymore, but I still know one of the names of the Americans -- that was a Lt. Mican, from New York.

Q   When were they caught, and how?

A   After the collapse of the insurrection they fled to the mountains of Lower Tatra. They were then captured by German police commandos.

-25-   Wisliceny

49

Q   Were they in Allied uniforms?

A   As far as I know, yes.

Q   When they were captured, where were they taken?

A   First they were brought to Bratislava.

Q   When was that?

A   The end of November or the beginning of December, 1944.

Q   And then what happened to them in Bratislava?

A   The Commander of the Security Police, Litiska sent a report about them to Himmler, to RSHA.

Q   Did the report go directly to Himmler or what kind of a route did it take?

A   It went to RSHA and from there to the department for the questions concerning Slovakia and the insurrection and then as a direct report to Himmler for a decision -- the way it is shown on the chart.

Q   What decision did Himmler make?

A   The members of this mission were supposed to be brought to Mauthausen.

Q   Was the order signed by Himmler?

A   Yes.

                         were
Q   And then they/brought there? What happened there in Mauthausen?

A   They were supposed to be interrogated there.

Q   By whom?

A   The interrogation was directed by Obersturmbann-fuehrer Schoneseiffen. The object of the interrogation was

to develop information on the organization of the American
and British intelligence services.

Q   Was Schoneseiffen the only one sent from
Berlin?

A   There were several people, but the rest of
them were (small) *MINOR* criminal (officials) *AGENTS* Schoneseiffen was the
chief interrogator.

Q   Did he speak English?

A   No.

Q   Who was interpreting?

A   That I could not tell. The court report was
signed by the interrogator and a statement to the effect that
it had been correctly translated was attached.

Q   Signed by the interrogator or the interrogate d?

A   Signed by both.

Q   Were there elaborate statements made there
by the prisoners?

A   Most of the members of the mission were only
signal men and ordinary soldiers. The officers who were
there were very thoroughly interrogated. That one could tell
from the minutes. Whether the interrogation was conducted
under stress and by force, one could not tell merely from the
minutes.

(Lt. Col. Brookhart returned to the room at this time.)

Q   Why do you say that? Have you heard something
to that effect?

A   That is quite possible, that such interrogations
were conducted by force.   -27-   Wisliceny

51

Q   You say that you could not see from the report that force had been used.

A   There were no remarks such as "signatures obtained under duress" or "signatures refused", or "just a moment!" I know for a fact that the court report on the chief of the American military mission was signed and the remark in English was "given under duress and protest" (witness writes words in English).   I know for certain that the word "duress" was there.

Q   Did you learn from other sources, not from the document, how the interrogations were conducted?

A   I want to emphasize that the time at my disposition for the study of these documents was very short. Schoneseiffen was inducted into active service on the 1st of February. I could only speak to him for a short time.

Q   Did he tell you anything about his mission to Mauthausen?

A   No, he didn't talk about this matter.

Q   The reports, you stated before, were quite detailed. How did you explain to yourself that they were so detailed?

A   There was an interrogation scheme and the questions that were to be asked of the witnesses were drawn up in great detail.

Q   Who prepared this questionnaire?

A   The questionnaire was prepared, first of all by Schoeneseiffen, himself, and also by Department 6 of the

Wisliceny

RSHA.

Q   And what part did Kaltenbrunner take in
sending down the special people from Berlin to Mauthausen?

A   He had nothing to do with the selection of
the interrogators and people sent to Mauthausen, but he was
currently informed of the proceedings there. The selection
was made by Gruppenfuehrer Mueller. Himmler himself was very
much interested in the proceedings dealing with the Anglo-
American military mission in Slovakia, and had to be informed
of the proceedings.

Q   Who informed him?

A   Kaltenbrunner informed him according to the
channels. Schoneseiffen prepared the report and it was then
submitted to Mueller, and from there to Kaltenbrunner and
finally a copy was given to Himmler.

Q   How do you know this?

A   I could tell that from the files because the
copies were always in the files.

Q   But you said earlier during our conversations
that in important matters, two copies were signed by the
chief. Was that the case here too? Did you see the copy
or the original signed by Kaltenbrunner?

-      A   In the files there were only the copies,
because the original went directly to Himmler.

Q   What happened to the members of the mission
in Mauthausen after the interrogation?

A   What I am going to say now I did not get out

53

of the files. The files were actually closed after the
interrogations. However, I learned the following from
a request by the OKW that they were trying to learn what
had happpened to the prisoners because they were supposed
to be turned over to the regular prisoner of war camps
after the interrogations. This request was attached to
the files. I read it. There must have been, however, some
other files or separate documents dealing with this case
which Schoenseiffen kept in his safe or had hidden away
for safekeeping.

Q   How do you come to this conclusion?

A   When on the 1st of February the files were to be
destroyed, I noticed that Schoenseiffen took out the file
on the American-Anglo military mission and added to it
several loose leaves from somewhere else. These documents
were not to be burned.

Q   What happened to the documents?

A   They were brought to Berlin.

Q   To whom?

A   Conditions were so confused at the time that
it is hard to keep track of what happened to these documents.
The most important documents were brought to Berlin and
probably to this department. I then heard that the members
of the Anglo-American mission were shot at Mauthausen.

Q   Who told you?

A   I believe that Obersturmbannfuehrer Tomsen. He
belonged to Section IVB2, which had Polish matters under

them. Tomsen told me during the course of my conversation with him that according to an order of Hitler, these members of the Anglo-American mission were shot as a measure of retribution.

Q   Who had brought the matter to Hitler's attention?

A   That went through the hands of Kaltenbrunner and Himmler.

Q   Do you deduce that because it was the regular channel, or do you know it for sure?

A   The channels were always adhered to in such cases. This one as well. Channels were always adhered to on orders and their execution. Channels were laid down in very definite rules. There was no by-passing of these regulations, but I cannot vouch for all of these things. I can only say what I heard in this conversation.

55

Q   Did you find an answer in the documents to the request of the OKW?

A   No, because the request of the OKW had been made about the middle of January, when conditions were already deteriorating, and this request was the last document, attached to these files.

Q   We will stop now.

APPROVED:

Smith W. Brookhart Jr.
INTERROGATOR

George A. Schlein
INTERPRETER

Thomas Jaynes
COURT REPORTER

- 32 -

TESTIMONY OF RUDOLF HOESS TAKEN
AT NURNBERG, GERMANY, ON 1 APRIL,
1946, 1430 to 1730 by Mr. Sender
Jaari and Lt. Whitney Harris.
Also present: Mr. George Sackheim,
Interpreter; Piilani A. Ahuna,
Court Reporter.

QUESTION BY MR. JAARI TO THE INTERPRETER:

Q Do you swear that you will fully and truly interpret
the testimony from German to English and English to German?

A I do.

QUESTIONS BY MR. JAARI TO THE WITNESS THROUGH THE INTERPRETER:

Q What is your name?

A Rudolf Hoess.

Doc. 3

56

Q Do you swear that you will tell the whole truth before
God?

A I do.

Q How old are you?

A 46 years old.

Q Where were you born?

A In Baden

Q Can you give me a very short description of your education and your eventual participation in the first world war.
Do you speak English?

A I understand some. I attended the Halzbach High School
in 1916. I volunteered for the calvary and spent two years in
Iraq and Palestine.

Q   What did you do after the war was finished?

A   After my return I joined the Frei Korps Rossbach in the Baltic.

Q   One moment - how long did you stay with the Frei Korps Rossbach?

A   From 1919 to 1921.

Q   You fought first in the Baltic?

A   In the Ruhr area and upper Silesia against the Red Army. There was an uprising...

Q   Do you mean a Communist uprising?

A. Yes.

Q   In upper Silesia against whom did you fight?

A   Against the Polish surgents.

Q   Until 1921?

A   Yes.

Q   And then?

A   And then I learned agriculture.

Q   Where?

A   In Silesia and Mecklenburg.

Q   And how long did that last?

A   Until 1923. Then in 1923 I was arrested because I participated in a Fehme killing.

Q   In Mecklenburg?

A   Yes.

Q   Who was murdered?

A   The man who denounced Schlageter to the French.

Q   And were you sentenced?

A   In 1924 I was convicted by the State Court in Leipzig

to ten years in the penitentiary.

Q Who had arranged the murder of Schlageter's denouncer?

A I have to state that briefly. The traitor was a member of Rossbach, and he eventually disappeared. He then reappeared in Mecklenburg at the time when there was the resistance against the French in the Ruhr area; and then he tried to hire men among the former members of the Rossbach Frei Korps to aid the French.

Q What do you mean by the expression "to aid the French"?

A The German railroad members refused to run the trains, and he wanted to hire people who would run the trains for the French.

Q That's your explanation?

A Yes.

Q I am not very interested in the details, as I want to know who made the decision that the man was to be murdered?

A We all arrived at this decision at Pranz in Mecklenburg at the time when we discovered from his papers and from his diary that he worked for the French and had betrayed Schlageter to the French.

Q Why did you search him?

A Because we wanted to know who he was working for and who was paying him.

Q Had members of the Rossbach Frei Korps groups around the country?

A Yes, I had such a group in Parshim consisting of twenty men.

Q Were you the leader of this group?

A Yes.

Q   From whom did you receive your orders?

A   From Rossbach the Frei Korps.

Q   When you say "Rossbach the Frei Corps" do you mean the organization Rossbach, or do you mean a man by the name of Rossbach?

A   The organization.

Q   Who was in charge of this organization?

A   That was the former Frei Korps Leader Rossbach.

QUESTIONS BY LT. HARRIS TO THE WITNESS THROUGH THE INTERPRETER:

Q   His name was Rossbach?

A   Yes.

QUESTIONS BY MR. JAARI TO THE WITNESS THROUGH THE INTERPRETER:

Q   Did you have a direct channel to him?

A   The Frei Corps had been disbanded and the remaining members had been divided into small groups and were working all over the countryside on farms.

Q   Did these groups have connections with the NSDAP?

A   No, only partly. The members were represented individually but they had no direct connection as groups.

Q   When did you join the party?

A   In November 1922.

Q   And the murder was committed in November 1923?

A   Yes.

Q   What negotiations did you have with party officials before this killing was committed?

A   That wasn't at all possible. He appeared suddenly and one or two hours later he was carried away.

59

Q   What position did you have in the party at that time?

A   I was only a member.

Q   Now you told us that you had been sentenced to ten years in the penitentiary. When were you released?

A   In 1928. After five years, I was granted a pardon.

Q   And what did you do then?

A   I returned to agriculture and joined the Atamanen - forerunner of the Hitler Youth Organization.

Q   Who was the leader of Atamanen?

A   Rosenberg.

Q   Who is Rosenberg?

A   Before him there were several others.

Q   And when did you join the SS?

60   A   In 1933.

Q   When in 1933?

A   In July or August.

Q   And you stayed with agriculture until 1933, didn't you?

A   I was always in agriculture.

Q   And what did you do after 1933?

A   In 1933, when I joined the SS, I was on an estate as a leader of an Atamanen group at the time the Reichs Fuehrer SS summoned me and sent me to Dachau.

Q   Did you know Himmler before that?

A   Yes. Himmler had also been a former member of the Atamanen.

-5-   HOESS

Q When did you meet him for the first time?

A I believe that was in 1930 or 1931. I cannot say exactly.

Q Did you know him intimately at that time?

A No, I met him at a meeting.

Q Buy why did he recall you in 1933 when he needed a man for Dachau?

A This was on the occasion of a parade at which I led a small SS Cavalry group, and it caught his attention and he called me and asked me what my plans were and then also asked me whether I wanted to join the administration of a concentration camp.

Q And your answer?

A I accepted, yes.

61

Q And what was your rank at that time?

A Scharfuehrer (NCO).

Q And upon your arrival in Dachau were you promoted?

A No.

Q And what were your duties?

A At first I participated in a military training program for six months.

Q Where?

A In Dachau with the SS.

Q Were there any army members NCO's or officers training you?

A No, the training personnel were members of the Bavarian Landespolizei.

Q And was Himmler Chief of the Landespolizei at that time?

A No, at that time he wasn't.

Q And when you had concluded your training course, what did you do then?

A Then I joined the actual concentration camp; that is, the protective custody camp.

Q In what capacity?

A As Prisoner Company Commander, as it was called at that time.

Q What were your duties as Prisoner Company Commander?

A I had a company of 270 prisoners whom it was my duty to supervise and take care of in their work at the camp.

Q The supervision of the camps, as for example your duties, did they all belong to the SS?

A Yes.

Q Was a certain group of the SS connected with your kind of duties.

A Yes, those were the SS Death Head Units.

Q And how long did you remain as company leader?

A One year.

Q The whole time in Dachau?

A Yes.

Q And what happened to you then?

A Then I became Rapport Leader; that is, the immediate supervisor of Prisoner Company Commanders.

Q Why were you promoted to that important position?

-7-   HOLSS

A I don't know that.

Q And then what was the next step in your promotions?

A And then I became SS Obersturmfuehrer, but that was subsequently.

Q And how long did you remain with this position?

A Until 1937.

Q And then?

A Then I became the administrator of prisoners property.

Q And this was all in Dachau?

A Yes.

Q And how long did you stay in that position?

A Until May 1938.

Q What happened then?

A And then I was transferred as adjutant to the Commanding
officer of Sachsenhausen Concentration Camp.

63

Q And how long did you stay in Sachsenhausen?

A I remained there for two years - until 1940.

Q You were not sent to the front in 1939 or 1940?

A No.

Q And what happened in 1940?

A In 1940 I was transferred as Camp Commander to
Auschwitz.

Q What month?

A On May 1, 1940.

Q Who appointed you?

A The Inspector of Concentration Camps Gruppenfuehrer
Gluecks.

-8-   HOESS

Q   But wasn't Pohl the Inspector of Concentration Camp?

A   At that time he was not.

Q   Was it a written order?

A   Yes.

Q   Signed by Gluecks?

A   Yes.

Q   And did it read on order of Reichs Fuehrer SS, or how did it read?

A   I was summoned to him and received oral instructions and then a written order was given me according to which I was supposed to establish a concentration camp in Upper Silesia.

Q   When you arrived, had construction started?

A   It was a former Polish artillery barracks and a few buildings were already there.

Q   Were there any inmates at the time of your arrival?

A   No, there was no one there.

Q   How large was the area which was assigned for this purpose?

A   Originally, it was only the actual Polish Military Camp.

Q   What was the name of the place where they were?

A   Auschwitz.

Q   And now you arrived; then you started to construct for the barracks, didn't you.

A. No, first I had to get the affairs of the camp in order. It had been neglected very much, and I had to repair several shot-up barracks. Only later did I have additional buildings constructed.

Q Who did the labor? Who were the actual people who did the labor?

A The work was done by concentration camp inmates; additional ones were coming all the time. To begin with, only thirty had come along from Sachsenhausen.

Q From where did the additional inmates arrive, and who were they?

A Kattowitz - from the Commander of the Security Police of Kattowitz.

Q Who was that?

A I do not know what his name was but later on it was the Oberfuehrer Bierkamp.

Q What nationalities were these inmates from Kattowitz?

A Only Poles.

Q Were they whole families, or were they only males?

A Only men.

Q How many Poles did you get from Kattowitz?/

A In the beginning there must have been - that is, until the end of 1940 - there were about 2,000 to 3,000 of them.

Q And that was all you got of inmates, or perhaps let us call them laborers, until the end of 1940?

A Yes, there were no more at that time?

Q And what was the development of the camp beginning in 1941?

A In January 1941 the figure rose appropriately and there were already 8,000 or 9,000 at that time.

-10-　　　　　　　HOESS

65

Q All Poles?

A Only Poles.

Q Now, please give us a chronological description, but contain yourself to facts and figures, of the development of the camp and the nationalities.

A In March or April 1941 the Reichs Fuehrer SS Himmler was there for an inspection.

Q Who accompanied him?

A The Gauleiter of Upper Silesia Bracht and the Regierungs-rat President and Gruppenfuehrer Karl Wolf who at that time was Himmler's adjutant. And then the Reichs Fuehrer had explained to him thoroughly maps about possible extensions to the camp.

Q Who gave the explanation?

A I did. And then the Reichs Fuehrer ordered that the camp was supposed to be greatly enlarged and the gauleiter who at that time was responsible for the agriculture development was supposed to put 20,000 morgens at the disposal of the camp for agriculture purposes.

Q From whom was the land taken?

A This whole area was between the Vistula and Sury Rivers. It was an area which was swampy and had a lot of underwater land. It consisted of seven villages which were inhabited by Poles who worked in Auschwitz in the factory and railroads.

Q What happened to the inhabitants of these seven villages?

A The inhabitants were resettled into the town of Auschwitz in so far as they were employes in the industries there.

HOESS

Q   And the others?

A   And the rest were returned to Poland to the general government.

Q   And what were your orders for the construction of new buildings on these 20,000 morgens?

A   The actual concentration camp was supposed to be enlarged to accommodate 30,000 prisoners and in the area of Birkenau a prisoner of war camp accommodating 100,000 prisoners of war was to be constructed.

Q   Was Birkenau between the area of Sury and Vistula?

A   Yes, it was two kilometers distance from the Auschwitz camp.

Q   The guards of this camp, were they also Death Heat Units?

A   Yes, all of them.

Q   No foreigners?

A   No, they only came later.

Q   And Camp Birkenau is the camp which later was known as Camp "B"?

A   No, Camp "B" was a division of Birkenau. Birkenau was divided into "A", "B", and "C" sectors.

Q   Did they ever assign prisoners of war to Birkenau?

A   No, only 10,000 Russian prisoners of war came to Auschwitz, and they constructed Birkenau.

Q   When they had finished the construction, what happened to them?

A   They always worked there. They remained there.

-12-   HOESS

Q   And they were still there when you left Birkenau in 1944?

A   Not all of those 10,000, but some prisoners of war were still there.

Q   Why weren't they all there?

A   A great many of them died from spotted fever or other epidemics. They had been undernourished when they arrived at the camp.

Q   So, if I understand you correctly, the plans according to the Reichsfuehrer SS were a concentration camp for 30,000 inmates in Auschwitz and 100,000 at Birkenau but only 10,000 prisoners ever arrived and they were used for construction work.

A   Yes.

68

Q   Who came to the camp designed for the 30,000 and when did they arrive?

A   That was always Poles from Upper Silesia, and the General government.

Q   Only males?

A   Yes, at the beginning only men but as of the middle and the end of 1941 there were women as well.

Q   And was the figure 30,000?

A   That was already in the summer of 1941. I couldn't accommodate all of 30,000 in Auschwitz because the barracks had not been completed; therefore, I had to send part of them to Birkenau.

Q   When were the Auschwitz camp facilities completed?

A   At the end of 1942 the camp facilities at Auschwitz had been completed.

HESS

Q   And the construction work in Auschwitz was still performed only by Poles?

A   Yes.

Q   And in Birkenau the Russians worked?

A   No, also Poles.

Q   And when was Birkenau completed?

A   That was never completed. Sector III had not been completed in 1944.

Q   So you were enlarging the camp then all the time?

A   During the entire years there was always construction going on.

Q   When did you start to receive other nationalities in Birkenau; I mean those other than Poles.

A   In the beginning of 1942 we began to get more inmates for Birkenau.

69

Q   Just let us stop for a moment and go back to 1941. By the end of 1941, as I understand you, you had in the whole area, the whole concentration camp area, 30,000 Poles and 10,000 Russians.

A   A total of 30,000 - that is, Russians and Poles together.

Q   You mean 20,000 Poles and 10,000 Russians.

A   Yes.

Q   Only males.

A   Yes, only men.

Q   But you said that you started to receive families by the end of 1941.

A   I said 30,000 males and in addition about 6,000 to 7,000 women. I don't know that exactly.

Q   Were they kept separately?

A   Yes.

Q   At first they were accommodated at Auschwitz and then?

A   And then in Birkenau subsequently.

Q   Now let's go back to the year 1942.

A   The development became more rapid and additional prisoners were arriving. In addition, there was the delivery of Jews which began in 1941 and then it was recommenced in the Spring of 1942.

Q   How many Jews did you receive in 1941?

A   I believe at that time we only received 6,000 Slovakian Jews.

Q   Are you sure about the figure?

A   It may have been 7,000. They were selected for their ability to work.

Q   Was this in addition to the figures you mentioned, or were they included in the figures you mentioned?

A   These are included in the figures I mentioned.

Q   And where did they work - in the factories or in the agriculture?

A   Many in agriculture.

Q   Then in the beginning of 1942 Jews started to arrive in greater numbers, didn't they?

-15-   HOESS

A Yes.

Q From where did they come?

A At first, from Poland; that is, the General Government from Germany, and I believe from Greece or Holland. I cannot tell the exact sequence and paralleled with that were shipments from France.

Q And this was in 1942?

A Yes, this continued until 1943, but I cannot remember the sequence of shipments.

Q How many did you get from the General Government of Poland?

A Approximately 250,000 is the figure I still remember. This includes Upper Silesia.

Q How many did you get from Greece?

A 65,000.

Q How many from Germany.

A We received 100,000, but I do not know exactly whether all of these came from Germany.

Q The transports went to a great degree through Teresienstadt?

A Yes.

Q And from Holland?

A 90,000.

Q And from France?

A From France 110,000.

Q From Slovakia?

A 90,000.

Q From Bulgaria?

A We did not get any.

HOESS

Q From what other countries did you receive Jews?

A From Belgium 20,000 and in the end from Hungary.

Q How many?

A 400,000.

Q Now you just told us you had facilities for 130,000. If you add all those figures they amount to a much greater number than 130,000. How could you accommodate all these people?

A They were not supposed to be employed in work there, but they were supposed to be exterminated.

Q You had decided that?

A That order I received in mid year of 1941, I believe it was July, from the Reichs Fuehrer SS in person.

Q Did you say 1941?

A Yes, 1941.

72

Q But you didn't mention before that any one of the Poles or Jews you received in 1941 were exterminated. Was anybody killed in 1941?

A You asked me about the expansion of Auschwitz, and I wanted to reserve this story of the killings for a separate set of questions.

Q Well, let's take it down that way. How many were killed in 1941 and what were their nationalities?

A I cannot give the figure, but the nationalities were Poles, Slovaks, and German Jews, but I cannot give you the total figure.

HOESS

Q   You didn't mention before that German Jews arrived in Auschwitz in 1941. Do you know for sure that German Jews were executed in 1941?

A   They could only have come from the Upper Silesian district.

Q   When you mentioned Poles before having arrived in Auschwitz in 1941, did you include Polish Jews?

A   Yes, they were included.

Q   By what means were they executed in 1941?

A   By gas.

Q   None by shooting?

A   No.

Q   None by hanging?

A   There were no shootings or hangings unless they had been condemned by the Standgericht; that is, the court of the Gestapo.

Q   Did you have a Standgericht in the camp?

A   No, I myself had no such court but the Standgericht of the Gestapo was always heard in Auschwitz.

Q   Do I understand you clearly that the Standgericht was heard in Auschwitz, or did you mean was it executed by the Standgericht and carried out in Auschwitz.

A   No, they actually held the court there.

Q   You used the word "Gestapo" in this connection. Was this Standgericht supervised or introduced by the Gestapo?

A   The Gestapo headquarters had its court meetings in Auschwitz and the Chief Judge was the Gauleiter.

Q   But you said you received the order from the Reichs Fuehrer SS in person.

A   Yes.

HOESS

73

Q About July 1941? Where did you see him?

A I was ordered to him in Berlin.

Q Are you sure it was after the Russian campaign had started.

A No, it was before the Russian campaign had started.

Q Then it couldn't have been in July.

A I cannot remember the exact month, but I know for sure it was before the date that the Russian campaign was launched.

Q Where did you meet him.

A In his office on Prince Albert Street 8.

Q Who else was present?

A I was alone.

Q What reasons did he give for this order?

A I don't recall his exact words, but the meaning was that the Fuehrer had given the order for the final solution of the Jewish problem.

Q What does final solution mean?

A That means the extermination; that's the way he stated it.

Q You state it as meaning the extermination?

A Yes.

Q Did you know the expression previous to that time?

A No, it appeared there for the first time.

Q Did he express himself that way? Did he explain to you what "final solution" meant?

A Yes, he explained it to me.

-19-   HOESS

Q   Was it a conception or a word which was known in the SS circles?

A   No, as I already said, this word appeared for the first time on that occasion. Later on, of course, I heard it repeatedly in 1942 and 1943 and then more was meant by that.

Q   Did he give you any detailed directives as to how the extermination was to take place?

A   Yes, he explained the following to me: the extermination camps in Poland that existed at that time were not capable of performing the work assigned to them.

Q   What were these extermination camps? Where were they, and what were their names?

A   There were three camps: first, Treblinka, Belzak near Lemberg and the third one was about 40 kilometers in the direction of Kulm. It was past Kulm in an easterly direction.)   75

Q   Under whose supervision were these three camps?

A   The commander of the Security Police.

Q   Do you mean SS?

A   In other words, the RSHA.

Q   What AMT of the RSHA supervised these camps?

A   I assume that it was the executive. I, myself, don't know it.

Q   Why didn't you know that?

A   I didn't have anything to do with the inspectorate of a concentration camp. I had nothing to do with these matters in this connection.

Q Are you talking about the extermination now?

A Yes.

Q But where did RSHA get into the picture?

A Because the SD and the Commander of the Security Police were under RSHA.

Q So, if I understand you correctly now, in the Gestapo there was a line of connection between the Gestapo and the Commander of the Security Police?

A Yes.

Q And they were responsible for the people who came to the camps in order to be exterminated?

76

A Who were they?

Q Would you then explain to me how it worked. Let me give you a couple of questions: Gluecks and Pohl were responsible for the administration and construction of camps, weren't they?

A Yes.

Q Who decided who was to be exterminated?

A The Reichsfuehrer Himmler.

Q But he could not have the time to make the decision in all these cases. Which one of his agencies worked on this problem?

A Department IV. That is, Gruppenfuehrer Mueller or his expert Hauptsturmbannfuehrer Eickmann.

Q In other words, the Gestapo?

A Yes, they decided who was to be delivered to the camps, who were to be employed as laborers and who were to be exterminated.

77

Q And who was Mueller's chief?

A His direct superior was Kaltenbrunner, the Chief of the RSHA.

Q And who was the chief before Kaltenbrunner?

A Heydrich.

Q And who was chief during the interval between Heydrich's death and Kaltenbrunner's appointment?

A I don't know for certain but whatever orders I saw during this time were signed by Gruppenfuehrer Mueller.

Q And after that they were signed by Kaltenbrunner?

HOESS

A No, I don't think you quite understand this. As far as I was concerned, concentration camps of any kind - with the exception of direct administration such as billeting, feeding - that was the duty of the Office of the Inspectorate of Concentration Camps, and the Chief Executive of AMT IV was Gruppenfuehrer Mueller.

Q When he signed his orders, did he sign them with the Roman IV?

A We hardly ever received original orders. We mostly received telegrams which were simply signed "Mueller." As far as I can remember, orders were signed "IV".

Q When he signed "IV", who was he signing for?

A He was signing for his Chief, that is, Kaltenbrunner. That is, he was always the deputy of the Chief of the RSHA.

Q Do you mean that he was the deputy of Kaltenbrunner?

A Yes, that's the way I mean it.

Q Did Mueller ever visit Auschwitz?

A No, never.

Q And Kaltenbrunner?

A No, never. I never saw it.

Q Did you ever meet Kaltenbrunner?

A Yes, on one occasion I met him personally in his office.

Q Did you report to him?

A That was already in 1944 when I had to report to him on Mauthausen. At the same time I was no longer Commandant but I was already Chief with the Inspectorate of Concentration Camps.

HOESS

Q Did AMT Chiefs in the Inspectorate of Concentration
Camps report to Kaltenbrunner?

A No, this was only a report of Mauthausen which I delivered
and at which time I represented Gruppenfuehrer Gluecks because I
had worked on this myself.

Q What was Kaltenbrunner's interest in that report?

A Because Kaltenbrunner had received this commission as a
result of a visit of Himmler in Mauthausen.

Q Was Himmler accompanied by Kaltenbrunner on this visit?

A I don't know that, but I assume that they met there.

Q What was it about? What was this report about?

A It dealt with the so-called "nameless people"; that is,
those who had already been condemned but had not as yet been
executed.

Q Why hadn't they been executed?

A I was just about to explain that. The Reichsfuehrer
said it was not right to execute these people because they were
young, strong and healthy and that they could work and that they
were to work at Mauthausen under a special guard. It then
happened that no work could be found for that many people;
that is, approximately from 400 to 500 in Mauthausen under heavy
guard. Therefore, it was my assignment to report on the fact
that they could be used in the armament industries working under-
ground in the vicinity of Mauthausen. Those were the contents of
the report I delivered to Kaltenbrunner.

Q And that was the first time you saw Kaltenbrunner?

-24-   HOESS

A Yes, that was the only time.

Q Let's return to Auschwitz - no, to Berlin where you just had discussed with Himmler the extermination of Jews in Auschwitz.

A Yes.

Q You told us that he gave you detailed oral orders, didn't you?

A Yes.

Q Who else did you discuss the details of extermination of Jews in Auschwitz with?

A I was not allowed to discuss this with anybody; it was a top secret matter.

Q Did Himmler give you orders about the construction of gas chambers?

A No, he told me the following: that I was supposed to look at an extermination camp in Poland and eliminate in the construction of my camp the mistakes and inefficiency existing in the Polish camp. I was supposed to show him plans of how I intended to construct my camp in a period of about four weeks. He told me that he could not give me the exact figures at that time, nor the numbers in which they would arrive, but added that the figure would run into several millions.

Q And what did you do?

A He explained to me that the most important matter was that when an action was being carried on in one of these countries it was not to be stopped or delayed because of

HOESS

inadequate facilities in Auschwitz. He told me that the camps
in Poland were not suitable for enlargement and the reason why
he had chosen Auschwitz was because of the fact that it had
good railroad connections and could be enlarged and was removed enough from centers of people and could be cut off from
connections with the people.

Q   And did he tell you anything else. Did you go there
immediately after your talk with him on your tour of inspection?

A   No, at first I returned to Auschwitz. He explained to
me that it was not his habit to discuss such matters with
inferiors; however, this case was so important and of such great
significance that he had decided to explain to me his reasons
and they were as follows: he said to me that if the extermination of Jewery did not take place at this time the German people
would be eliminated by the Jews.

Q   Did he explain to you how the Jews would be able to
eliminate the German people?

A   No.

Q   What other reasons did he give?

A   That was the reason. He had planned originally to
dispatch a higher ranking officer to Auschwitz to continue
this extermination action, but reconsidered because he felt
that it would only be a cause of friction between myself as the
Camp Commandant and the higher ranking officer in charge of the
exterminations. Therefore, he gave me the order. In addition
to that the fact that 1 was supposed to treat this as top

-26-   HOESS

secret matter and not discuss it with anybody was explained.
All the instructions such as procedure and orders I was to
receive from the RSHA through Eichmann.

Q   And then before you went on your tour of inspection
you returned to Auschwitz?

A   Yes.

Q   What did you do in Auschwitz?

A   I immediately got in touch with the chief of a
construction unit and told him that I needed a large crematorium.
I told him that we were going to receive a large number of sick
people, but I did not give him my real reason.

Q   And then?

A   And after we had completed our plans, I sent them to
the Reichsfuehrer. After I had changed them in accordance with
the real purpose of his instructions, they were approved.

Q   Didn't you visit any of the three existing extermination camps?

A   Yes.

Q   Which ones?

A   Treblinka....

Q   What did you see there?

A   At that time the action in connection with the Warsaw
Ghetto was in progress, and I watched the procedure.

Q   How was it done there?

A   They had chambers for about 200 people. Into these

chambers the fumes from an exhaust machine came in. These motors had been taken from captured enemy equipment such as tanks, trucks and had been installed next to the gas chambers. They were run by gas, and those victims were supposed to be suffocated by the fumes.

Q   How many chambers were there, and how many people were killed?

A   I do not know the exact figure, but there may have been about ten chambers. It was built next to a ramp and the train drove right up to it. The people were unloaded right into the chambers, and this procedure was necessary because the motors did not always work right.

Q   Weren't the people first registered or interrogated?

A   No.

Q   They were put directly into the chambers from the trains?

A   Yes.

Q   And what happened to their clothing?

A   They had to undress before they were put into the chambers.

Q   And their valuables?

A   That was all sorted. I saw a number of shacks there in which there were piles of clothing, shoes, valuables, etc., all sorted separately and neatly stacked. They were later packed.

Q   What happened to these things?

A   I do not know.

Q   Who did the sorting?

A   Inmates.

Q   Who guarded the trains in which the Jews were to be gassed alive?

A   The train that I saw in Treblinka arrived guarded by members of the Security Police; also the trains that came into Auschwitz from Poland were guarded by the Security Police.

Q   Did the train loads consist of women, men and children all together?

A   All together.

Q   We are now talking about the train in Treblinka?

A   Yes, the one in Treblinka.

Q   Were there babies, real small children and very old people also?

84

A   All kinds, if they were evacuated from Warsaw.

Q   You only saw one train in Treblinka during your visit there?

A   Yes, only one.

Q   How many people were in that train?

A   One train generally handled 2,000 people.

Q   When you said generally, do you mean that the trains arriving in Auschwitz also usually had 2,000 people?

A   Yes, 2,000 on an average. Some trains held 2,400; others, 1,500 and 1,800 but the average was 2,000.

Q   Was this the first time that you observed exterminations?

A   Yes.

Q   Now I understand from your statement that the people –
men, women and children had to strip themselves completely naked,
am I right?

A   Yes.

Q   And the women carried their babies with them into the
chambers?

A   Yes.

Q   And they knew what was going to happen to them?

A   Yes, I assume so.

Q   Did they know what was going to happen to them?

A   Yes, they did.

Q   And what was your reaction?

A   I did not consider this problem, or the means, or
the manner in which it was conducted because in my opinion they
knew it was going to happen to them.

85

Q   But you found it lawful and right that they were to
be exterminated. It was only the manner you objected to?

A   Yes, according to my discussions with Himmler it was
the way you just stated.

Q   Did anyone try to escape?

A   No, I didn't see that.)

Q   How long did you remain in Treblinka?

A   About three or four hours.

Q   Did you discuss the matter with the Camp Commandant
in Treblinka?

A   Yes.

Q   Who was he?

A   I don't remember his name.

-30-   HOESS

Q   Just one moment. How did you get into the camp?
What kind of a pass or permit did you have?

A   I was introduced by Eichmann. They had been advised
of my arrival by Eichmann.

Q   Was Eichmann with you?

A   No.

Q   Did you see Eichmann in Berlin beforeyou left?

A   Eichmann had been in Auschwitz in the meantime and
at that time I told him that I had to see this camp and that he
should advise them of my coming. Otherwise, I would not be able
to get into the camp.

Q   Did Eichmann have the power to let anyone visit the
camp?

86

A   No I don't believe so.

Q   How could he get you the orders to get in?

A   I assume that he had already received instructions
from the Reichsfuehrer via Gruppenfuehrer Mueller.

Q   While he was visiting you in Auschwitz did you discuss the plans with him?

A   Yes.

Q   Then he was completely in the know?

A   Yes.

Q   Didn't he want to go with you to Treblinka?

A   No, he returned to Berlin.

Q   Did he take the plans with him?

A   No

HOESS

Q   How did you send the plans to Himmler?

A   By courier.

Q   Directly to Himmler?

A   Yes, personally.

Q   You didn't approve of the methods used in Treblinka, so you made up your mind to improve these methods. What methods were you going to use?

A   I wanted to avoid, in any case, that the persons who came into Auschwitz should know ahead of time that they were going to be gassed.

Q   How did you plan to avoid that?

A   At the beginning I had to improvise because I didn't have the necessary buildings. Signs were installed reading "To Delousing" "To Disinfecting" "To Bath" "To the Showers", etc. In addition to that, inmates helped the new arrivals with undressing and gave them instructions as to where they were to place their clothing so that they would find it upon their return. It was done in order to avoid exciting them in any way or to give them an inkling of actually what was going to happen.

Q   And after the undressing, where did the victims go?

A   They went into these rooms.

Q   What rooms?

Q   These chambers. At first there were two old farms before the crematoriums were built. They were made airproof. The windows were shut by cement and air proof doors were constructed and in every chamber there was a small hole through which the gas was blown in.

-32-   HOESS

87

QUESTIONS BY LT. HARRIS TO THE WITNESS THROUGH THE INTERPRETER:

Q   What kind of gas was used?

A   Cyclone B. It was a crystal-like substance.

Q   From where did you receive these crystals?

A   Originally, this Cyclone B was used in order to gas rooms and to exterminate insects. Since it was very poison-ous and had to be treated with great care we assumed that it was the proper thing to use against humans.

Q   Was it long before the human beings were killed by this gas?

A   It depended on weather, humidity, time of day, and the number of people present in the chamber. Also, the gas was not always composed the same way and was not as effective every time.

QUESTIONS BY MR. JAARI TO THE WITNESS THROUGH THE INTERPRETER:

Q   In general, how long a time did it take?

A   I saw it happen often enough. Generally it took from three to fifteen minutes. The effect varied. Wherever the gas was thrown into the chamber, the people standing right next to it were immediately anaesthetized. It gradually spread out to the far corners of the room and generally after five minutes one could no longer discern the human forms in the chamber. Everybody was dead after fifteen minutes, and the chambers were opened after a half an hour and not once was anybody alive at that time.

Q   How were you able to hear voices from the chambers if they were so air-proof, as you said before?

HOESS

A   They were air-tight, but the walls were not too thick. They were only ordinary walls.

Q   So what noises did you hear while you were standing outside?

A   At first they all screamed, of course.

Q   Did you have any observation windows?

A   In the chambers made up out of the farm houses we did not have any but later on in the concrete crematorium we did.

Q   Who delivered the gas to you?

A   A gas company in Hamburg.

Q   To whom were the shipments of this gas addressed?

AO To the Administration of the Concentration Camp, Auschwitz.

Q   Who paid them?

A   I do not know, but I assume the Administration paid for it. I am sure they were paid.

Q   When was the construction of the permanent gas chambers finished?

A   All four were finished in 1943. We were already functioning in 1942.

Q   When in 1942 was the first one put into use? It was there already, perhaps, in November of 1941?

A   No, 1942.

Q   So these gas chambers, the provincial gas chambers, were used from the summer of 1941 up until 1942.

A   November of 1942. They were also used later on whenever the crematoriums were insufficient to handle the work.

-34-   HOESS

Q   How big were the chambers in the crematorium?

A   They could accommodate 2,000 persons.

Q   Each?

A   Yes, each.

Q   When the people arrived in Auschwitz, there was a railroad station within the camp already, wasn't there?

A   Yes.

Q   They were unloaded, and were they marched?

A   In this railroad station there was a side track. The people stepped down from the train, discarded their baggage and were then examined by doctors and sorted.

Q   Who were the doctors? What kind of dictors did you use?

A   The SS camp physicians.

Q   According to what principles were they sorted out?

A   According to the principles of whether they were fit for work or not.

Q   Now you say a trainload consisted on the average of 2,000 people. How many doctors did you have assigned to check on each trainload?

A   There were always two doctors on duty.

Q   How many trains arrived daily?

A   The largest number of trains that ever arrived in one day were five. This was in 1944 during the Hungarian action.

-35-   HOESS

Q   But on the average how many trains arrived daily?

A   Two.

Q   4,000 people?

A   Yes.

Q   And two doctors examined them?

A   Yes, they filed by them.

Q   So the examination really never took place; they
just had a look?

A   Yes.

Q   And according to which plan was the decision taken?

A   According to the order as to whether or not a man or
a woman was strong and healthy.

Q   And what about the children? Were all the children
killed?

A   That depended upon their stature.   Some of the 15 and   91
16-year old children also went to work, if they were strong.

Q   In other words, children below 15 were exterminated.

A   Yes.

Q   Just because of Himmler's order?

A   Yes.

Q   And because they were dangerous to the German people?

A   Yes.

Q   So a child of three or four years old was dangerous
to the German people.

A   No, it isn't quite that way. I should have elaborated perhaps a little more on my statement before of Himmler's explanation. He said the German people would not have carried rights unless the Jewish people were now exterminated.

Q   So that is really a confirmation of what you said. The German people could not rise at all because of the four-year old Jewish children.

A   Yes.

Q   In general, what was the percentage of the number of people killed and the number of people used for labor?

A   It varied between 20 and 30% that were set aside for work.

Q   And was this the percentage with men and women inclusively?

A   There were always more men fit for labor than women.

Q   Just to take an example, when you received the 65,000 Jews from Greece, how many of them were found fit for labor?

A   The Greeks were very ill and arrived in a very bad condition so that I believe the percentage in this case was approximately 15%.

Q   Right now, let's go back to the procedure at Auschwitz; they arrived, they had been what you call inspected by the SS doctors, one row was marched into the camp and they were the ones who were fit for labor, is that right?

A   Yes.

-37-   HOESS

Q   And the other row was marched into the farm houses?

A   Yes.

Q   Where they undressed?

A   Next to where they undressed in separate shacks next to the farm houses. Later on, in inclement weather other military barracks were constructed for them.

Q   And then?

A   And then They were separated according to sizes and marched in groups into the chambers.

Q   Groups of 200?

A   Yes.

Q   And the people who remained outside, could they hear what was going on in the two farm houses?

A   No.

Q   How many people could be accommodated in each farm house for extermination?

A   The farm houses accommodated in their various chambers one complete train shipment all at once.

Q   You told us that after one half hour the doors were opened?

A   Yes.

Q   Who removed the bodies?

A   A commando that worked there. It was primarily a commando of inmates.

Q   And where were the bodies taken?

-38-   HOESS

A   Behind the farm houses there were open pits in which
the bodies were burned.

Q   Who took care of the burning?

A   The same commando took care of all these duties.

Q   And when three trains arrived a day and the first
trainload was taken care of was the second train set on the
side track until every trace of the first trainload had been
removed?

A   Yes, two trainloads could be taken care of at the
same time in the two farm houses. In case a third train arrived
too early, it had to wait on the side track.

Q   Who removed bodies from the trains when they arrived.
I understand that there were bodies in the trains when they
arrived.

94

A   That was another commando of inmates who took care of
that work. They would be put on a truck and thrown into these
pits where they were burned.

Q   How many were generally dead? How many of the passen-
gers were already dead upon arrival?

A   That depended on where the train originally c ame
from and how long they had been on their way. In the case of
the Greek Jews who had been ten days in transit over 100 had died
on the way.

Q   And what about the Hungarian?

A   There were more.

Q   How many more?

-39-   HOESS

A   They varied. Sometimes the trains were composed of different parts. Sometimes a hospital had been put on to a train. In that case, of course, there were many more dead than when the trainload was from an agricultrual region.

Q   Do you know whether or not bodies were removed from the trains while in transit?

A   I never heard of that.

Q   And these bodies, before they were thrown on the fires, was their clothing taken off?

A   Yes.

Q   By your inmates?

A   Yes.

Q   What happened to the gold from the mouths of the victims?

A   That was melted.

Q   That I can understand, but was it removed from the victims before execution or after execution?

A   They were removed from the bodies before they were taken to the pits to be burned.

Q   Who did that? Who removed the gold?

A   There were among these commandos of inmates a few dentists.

Q   Who supervised their work?

A   The dental work was supervised by an SS Dentist whose duty it was to see that the work was done in a satisfactory manner.

Q   And when did the victims take off their rings, bracelets, ear rings, etc.?

A   They took that off at the time when they got undressed with the exception of rings, which they kept on when
they went into the gas chambers. Those were removed after the
bodies were removed from the gas chambers.

Q   Just a moment - returning to the dental work, were
their gold teeth pulled out?

A   Yes.

Q   Did you have any complaints from the surrounding
villages about the smell from these pits?

A   When there was an Eastern wind the smell could be
noticed across the Vistula.

Q   And you received complaints from the Poles?

A   No, they didn't complain; it was only discussed
among the population but they did not complain.

Q   Well, this will be all for today.   )

- - - - - - - - -

APPROVED:

_____
INTERROGATOR

_____
INTERPRETER

_____
COURT REPORTER

Testimony of RUDOLF HOESS, taken at Nurnberg,

Germany, 2 April 1946, 1000 to 1230, by Mr.

S. Jaari, Interrogator.   Also present: Mr.

Leo Katz, Interpreter, and Charles J. Gallagher,

Court Reporter.

QUESTIONS BY MR. JAARI TO MR. KATZ:

Q   Do you solemnly swear that you will truly and faithfully translate my questions from English to German, and the responses of the witness from German into English to the best of your ability, so help you God?

A   I do.

QUESTIONS BY MR. JAARI TO THE WITNESS THROUGH THE INTERPRETER:

Q   Are you the same Rudolf Hoess who appeared for interrogation yesterday afternoon?

A   Yes.

Q   You understand your statements are still made under oath?

A   Yes.

Q   You understand your statements are still made under oath?

A   Yes.

Q   Yesterday afternoon we finished with your description of the procedure of gassing before the permanent crematoriums were constructed, didn't we?

A   Yes.

Q   And if I remember correctly you said that the gassings took place in Auschwitz in the two farm houses until the end of 1942?

A   Yes, but in the meantime one permanent crematorium was finished.

Q   When?

A   This was already finished a little before that time, about October 1942, so that they conducted this partly in the crematorium, and partly in

1   HOESS

the farm houses, but there was no definite separation.

Q   Before we go into the chronological order of happenings in Auschwitz, let me ask you if this statement given by you on 20 March, 1946, No. D-479B, in Minden Jail in Germany, is correct?

A   Yes, this is correct.

Q   This statement No. D749B, refers to how many members of the Waffen SS have served in Auschwitz, and you mentioned that approximately 7000 men of the Waffen SS have served at one time or the other at concentration camps, is that correct?

A   During the whole time, 7000 people at one time or another.

Q   You say that you were commandant of the concentration camp until the 1st of December, 1943?

A   Yes.

Q   Were not you there until 1944?

A   I was again in 1944 for two months in Auschwitz in order to introduce a new commandant there.

Q   When was that?

A   That was during the three months, June, July and August, 1944.

Q   What was the name of the new commandant?

A   After I left, this camp was split up into three different camps, and the three new commandants that I introduced were Sturmbannfuehrer Baer, Hauptsturm-fuehrer Kramer and Hauptsturmfuehrer Schwarz.

Q   And who was in charge between the 1st of December 1943 until June 1944?

A   Camp No. 1 Obersturmbannfuehrer Liebehenschel; camp No. 2 Sturm-bannfuehrer Hartjenstein, and, camp No. 3, it was Schwarz who remained after-wards.

Q   Now during the period until the first permanent plants were finished, how many human beings were gassed?

HOESS.

A   I cannot give you the number. I don't know.   Cannot even give you an estimate.

Q   How many were gassed daily?

A   As I already mentioned, if an operation was being undertaken, normally daily two trains were taken, that is to say 1600 to 1700 human beings were selected according to the various considerations and percentages that I mentioned to you yesterday.

Q   If I understand you correctly, you told me that one trainload consisted of 2000 people?

A   Yes.

Q   And two trains make four-thousand people, is that right?

A   Yes, sir.

Q   And even if we use a percentage of twenty-five percent able bodied men, that means one-thousand.

A   You should have understood me to mean on train of 1600 or 1700 people,   99
and then two trains would mean twice that number, and that would be 3400 altogether, or, 3500.

Q   So you mean that out of two daily trainloads about 3500 persons were gassed?

A   Yes, sir.

Q   Were you sure of that percentage, too?

A   Yes, and in the manner in which the trains came in.

Q   So you started such actions about July, 1941, didn't you?

A   Yes.

Q   From July 1941 to October 1942, that is fifteen months?

A   Yes.

Q   And the average, taking it very conservatively, was three-thousand people a day?

3   HOESS.

A   Yes, but these operations were not carried out daily, but they were carried out only until one of these operations was finished. For instance, four or five weeks, and then again for a period of time nothing was undertaken.

Q   So in 1941 you carried out actions against the Slovakians, and the Polish Jews?

A   Yes.

Q   How many?

A   I can only give you the final total. I do not know in what period of time they were being gassed.

Q   I had the figures yesterday, and we will return to them later. I am sure you forget yesterday to mention the Russian prisoners who were exterminated in Auschwitz?

A   Yes, I forgot. I did not mention it.

100   Q   Yesterday you told me only Jews were killed there.

A   The way you put the question to me, I took it to mean that you were only asking about Jews, and about the decision and sentence that had been passed by the SS Standgerichte, which were not added to these numbers.

Q   You told me yesterday that the executions caused by the SS Standgerichte sentence were carried out through hanging and shooting, and not by gassing; however, we know for certain that the Russian prisoners also were gassed, is that right?

A   Yes, but this has nothing to do with the sentence passed by the SS Standgerichte.

Q   But do you consider Russians as human beings, and Jews as cattle when you were talking about cattle executions yesterday, and not human executions?

- 4 -

HOESS

A   I assumed yesterday that you only wanted information about the execution of Jews, and not about the Russians.

Q   I want to know everything you can tell about every execution in Auschwitz, and I do not want you to hide anything from me.

A   Yes, I understand.

Q   Now we will have to go back to 1941, and find out how many Russian prisoners of war were gassed in Auschwitz in 1941.

A   I cannot give you this number.

Q   Approximately how many?

A   (No answer)

Q   Was it fifty-thousand?

A   No, not that many.   Perhaps ten-thousand.

Q   And was the procedure the same as when the Jews were gassed?

A   Yes.

101

Q   Who gave the order for the execution of the Russian prisoners of war?

A   These shipments came over the competent Stapo Agencies in Kattowitz, Troppau and Breslau.

Q   You knew that the prisoners of war were under the jurisdiction of SS,Gestapo?

A   I do not know that. They were transferred and turned over to the Stapo agency as prisoners of war. I do not know for what reason.

Q   Who selected them from their regular PW camps?

A   I do not know.

Q   The prisoners of war who came there, were they Russians, or were they from Turkestan, or were they all kinds of nationalities from USSR?

A   From what I saw of the people that arrived there, they were from all regions and areas of Russia.

Q   Who guarded them when they came?

A   Wehrmacht transport details brought them from the prisoner of war camps.

Q   Let's get this straight. Were they brought directly by members of the Gestapo from the PW camps, and under guard of Wehrmacht commandos to Auschwitz?

A   An officer of the Wehrmacht was commandant of the train, and the officer of the Gestapo had a letter of authorization from the Gestapo agency that these people in that train were to be given "special treatment."

Q   Who signed that order?

A   A competent Stapo chief from Kattowitz, from Troppau, or from Breslau, from whatever region these prisoners came.

Q   Did they come in a train, or did they march to Auschwitz?

A   In a train.

Q   How many prisoners were in each train?

A   Just the same as in the case of Jews, about two thousand.

Q   How large was the guard detail?

A   About a company's strength.

Q   Under the command of an officer?

A   Yes, a Wehrmacht officer.

Q   And N.C.O.S.?

A   Yes, also.

Q   The train arrived where in Auschwitz?

A   In the camp itself. We had a spur in the camp where the train arrived.

Q   Then what happened, were these prisoners marched out of the train directly into the gas chambers?

A   No, first the train was unloaded, and then after the train was unloaded th guard detail left the camp.

Q   Did not any representative of the Wehrmacht remain there to observe

102

- 6 -

HOESS

the proceedings, and see to it that the orders were carried out?

A   No, he probably had nothing to do with that. He was only concerned with the transporting of the prisoners from the prisoner of war camp to the concentration camp. The execution of the orders were matters of the Gestapo official.

Q   The Wehrmacht soldiers who took part in the guarding, did they know what was going to happen to the Russian PW's?

A   I don't believe that.

Q   Why don't you believe that?

A   Because it also happened that prisoners of war who were turned over to the camp arrived in trains for purpose of labor commitment.

Q   But it was known that the Auschwitz camp was not a PW camp, was not it?

A   Yes, that was generally known.

Q   Why were Russian PW's sent over to the camp? What did the soldiers think?

A   Perhaps, that they were also being used for labor purposes there.

Q   Were there ever any Wehrmacht officers, or members of the Wehrmacht in the camp who saw any proceedings there?

103

A   No, nobody was permitted in. The place where that train arrived was blocked off, and after the train was unloaded, the members of the Wehrmacht had to get back in the train, and they were not permitted in the area of the camp.

Q   How many years did the gassing of the Russian PW's continue?

A   I believe that this terminated with the beginning of 1942. As a matter of fact, I believe that we received no more prisoners of war after that period.

Q   You estimated about 10,000 PW's were killed in 1941?

- 7 -

HOESS

A   Yes.

Q   How many were killed in 1942?

A   I cannot give you any numbers. When I was interrogated at Minden, the interrogator told me that the total number certainly must have been somewhere in the neighborhood of 100,000, but I said that I did not think they were that many, that is impossible; that there was certainly not that many, but I always stress the fact I cannot give any definite figures.

Q   How about an estimate?

A   I do not believe that even a figure of 70,000 is possible.   I don't believe there were so many because the trains did not arrive every week, sometime there were no trains for weeks. I have tried to recall by counting by the months the total number of PW's who arrived there.

Q   What would your most conservative estimate be?

104   A   The most which is possible, estimating a period of about one year, is about eighteen to twenty-thousand.

Q   Including the ten-thousand in 1941, or exclusive of them?

A   This includes the ten-thousand in one year. But it does not include those ten-thousand that were turned over to us for labor purposes.

Q   So eighteen to twenty-thousand Russian PW's were gassed in Auschwitz?

A   Yes.

Q   How many were hanged?

A   Only those individual cases that were sentenced by the SS Standgerichte; they were only a few individual cases. They were either hanged or shot.

Q   What do you mean by a few cases?

HOESS

A   Perhaps two or three during the course of a month; there were only those who had committed a crime, or, attempted to steal while escaping.

Q   So Russian PW8s who attempted to flee, they were hanged?

A   No, those who had committed crimes, such as after a successful escape, that while escaping they had committed a crime, such as robbery or rape, and they were hanged.

Q   What happened to PW's who were recaptured and had not committed robbery or rape?

A   They were turned over to us as regular prisoners of the concentration camp for purposes of labor, and this happened frequently.

Q   Do you mean prisoners of a concentration camp, or a regular concentration camp internee placed in special rooms for inmates of a concentration camp?

A   The ones that came under the rules of concentration camps.

Q   And what happened when inspectors of the PWs, who were under the OKW, came to the camp on their regular inspections?

A   None arrived.

Q   Or when representatives from the International Red Cross came?

A   Never arrived in Auschwitz.

Q   Do you know that according to rules of war PWs are under the supervision of the International Red Cross?

A   Yes, I do.

Q   Didn't you ever contemplate why they did not inspect your camp?

A   According to my opinion they were no longer to be regarded as prisoners of war if they were turned over to the concentration camp by the Gestapo Agency.

Q   Didn't you ever think of it?

A   Yes, and as a matter of fact we were always told that the Russians did not recognize the regulations, and the agreements made by the International

HOESS

Red Cross or the Geneva Convention.

Q   So you were of the opinion that human beings who had fought against you could be treated just like cattle?

A   No.

Q   Was the treatment in the concentration camps well conducted?

A   How do you mean, good.

Q   Did they get enough to eat?

A   Yes.

Q   Did they have nice comfortable billets, just like your own soldiers?

A   No.

Q   But according to the rules regarding prisoners of war, they supposedly were to have the same kind of billets, and the same kind of food as the soldiers

A   Yes.

Q   Did they receive that?

106

A   No, this could not be. The received the same food, and the same billets as the other concentration camp inmates.

Q   Was that sufficient?

A   The food?

Q   Yes, was it enough?

A   Yes, the food, I would assume.

Q   How could you only assume such things. You were the commandant of Auschwitz, and you ought to know if they had enough to eat?

A   In the beginning when the food situation in Germany was still good, the food in the camp was completely sufficient, and adequate, but later, in 1943, whe the food situation became worse in Germany, and when also the prisoners in the camp increase, it was no longer possible for competent food agencies to have the necessary food, so that the prisoners could be fed properly.

Q   You are not telling the truth, Hoess. Already in 1941 great numbers of Russian PWs in concentration camps, and the inmates, died because of starvation.

A   No, I do not believe they died of malnutrition. They died of the diseases.

Q   But the epidemics were so great because the prisoners had no power of resistance; they were weak because of malnutrition, were not they?

A   Yes, that is correct. But the food was such that they could become satisfied. The calories of nutritional value in the food was probably not such that a man could withstand disease, such as typhus and typhoid.

Q   So that the sanitary conditions in the camp were very bad, because the epidemic could gain such a large scale foothold, weren't they?

A   In 1941 the sanitary equipment and institutions were still adequate and good. Then they became worse because of the increase in the prisoners, and the executions could not keep pace with them, and, also that the sanitary institutions and conditions could not be improved sufficiently fast.

107

Q   We will leave this topic for a moment, and go back to October, 1942, when the first permanent plants had been installed? .

A   Yes.

Q   Where were the plants located?

A   In Birkenau.

Q   And there was a spur leading up to the plants?

A   Yes.

Q   Now, when the train arrived the prisoners were unloaded just as

11

HOESS

they were unloaded during the previous executions?

A   Yes

Q   Then, where did they march?

A   Then those who were fit for labor were selected, and the others marched to this newly erected crematorium.

Q   Did the selecting of the able bodied Jews take place in the building, or outside?

A   Outside as before mentioned when the train arrived.

Q   That is, the Jews marched past the two SS doctors?

A   Yes.

Q   So, when a train with two thousand persons arrived, two thousand marched past the two doctors, and they just nodded, this one to labor and this one to the plant.

108 A   Yes.

Q   What kind of an examination was that. Was that a sufficient examination?

A   Yes, the doctors said that was sufficient.

Q   Were they real high-classed doctors?

A   Not all of them. There were a lot of doctors around.

Q   They must have been exceedingly clever, just to look at persons dressed up and still being able to say, "He is good and this other one is a bad one."

A   Yes, that is the way in which it was done.

Q   Have you ever been examined by a doctor for military duty?

A   Yes.

Q   Did he just take a glance at you, and then say that you were OK?

A   No.

Q   What did he do to examine you?

A   I had to undress, and was closely examined, my heart, lungs and other

12

HOESS

organs.

Q   Did not it ever enter your mind that the people that you were to employ in your war industries, and in your factories should be perfect specimens of manhood, physically strong and able bodied persons?

A   Only those who appeared at first glance to be strong and healthy were selected.

Q   How long did a laborer last, on an average?

A   That depended where he worked and at what he worked.

Q   How many hours a day did he work?

A   In an armament industry, ten hours. It also depended on the route of march from the place where they were housed. Also whether they did outside or inside work, and also whether they worked in subterranean rooms.

Q   And how much food did such a worker receive?

A   Those who worked in permanent industries received a normal food ration from the economic office, and they also received an additional supply of bread rations.

Q   Did they receive the same food as the Guards?

A   No, the guards were fed according to military rations, and the prisoners were fed civilian rations.

Q   But the prisoners quota was so large that it did not matter whether or not workers survived?

A   No, that is not correct. No, I was reprimanded repeatedly by my superior authority, OGRU Fu Pohl, who complained that not enough workers or men fit for labor were selected and used for labor purposes.

Q   But on the other hand you received complaints from Mueller and Eichmann that not enough were executed, didn't you?

A   Yes, that is correct, that was the opposition, or contrast.

Q   Which point of view won?

109

A   Pohl won, because the armament industry needed so many men that it was made a duty of every camp commandant, no matter where he was, to preserve as many labors as possible for purposes of labor.

Q   But still Auschwitz succeeded in exterminating quite a number, something like in the millions, didn't they?

A   Yes.

Q   How many millions?

A   I again refer back to the statement made to me by Eichmann in March or April, 1944, when he had to go and report to Reichfuehrer that his offices had turned over two and one-half million to the camp.

Q   To the Auschwitz area?

A   Yes.

Q   Only in the Auschwitz area?

A   Yes.

Q   Two and one-half million, you say?

A   Yes.

Q   Are yout you a little confused just now?

A   The reasons why I remember the number, two and one-half million, is because it was repeatedly told to me that Auschwitz was to have exterminated four or five million, but that was not so. We had an order by the Reichsfuehrer of SS to destroy all materials in numbers immediately, and not to preserve any records of the executions that were being carried out.

Q   The two and one-half million were people delivered to Auschwitz, were they the ones that were executed?

A   Executed and exterminated.

Q   Then quite a number more were delivered to the camp of Auschwitz?

A   Yes. According to the percentage that I have already mentioned,

14

HOESS

you would have to add twenty to thirty percent, who were used for labor purposes.

Q   Were these two and one-half million gassed?

A   Yes.

Q   And how about the half of million, which were put to death by other means?

A   They were those who died from diseases, and who perished by other sicknesses in the camp.

Q   Didn't you know what was going on in Auschwitz up until the last moment even when you had left your position as commandant?

A   Yes.

Q   You were with the administration and economic office, weren't you?

A   That is with the superior authority.

Q   So you were promoted from commandant of Auschwitz to what?

A   As chief of an Amt, or a department. In one of the departments as inspector of concentration camp.

Q   Was it Amt Vl?

A   That was in the Economic Amt Group D, in the economic and administration main office. That is, Amt Group entitled "Inspectorate of Concentration Camps."

Q   The people who were to be gassed in the permanent plants undressed in the free outside these large buildings, didn't they?

A   No, there was a special room.

Q   Just a moment ago you said they were undressed in the free outside?

A   No. The train was unloaded, they deposited their baggage, they were sorted out according to those fit for labor, and then the ones who had been selected marched away, and all the others undressed in an undressing room.

15

HOESS

Q   What was told would happen to them there?

A   They were told that they were going to be conditioned to take a bath, and to be deloused and disinfected, and the signs were there corresponding to these institutions..

Q   They undressed and put their things away just the same way you told us yesterday, as it would happen in the farm houses?

A   Yes.

Q   How many people could be gassed at the same time in one of the chambers in a permanent plant?

A   In one chamber, two thousand.

Q   A whole train load?

A   Yes.

Q   And how did the gassing take place?

A   It was all below ground. In the ceiling of these gas chambers, there were three or four openings that were fenced around with a grating that reached to the floor of the gas chamber, and through these openings the gas was poured into the gas chambers.

Q   And then what happened?

A   The same thing happened as I already told you happened in the farm houses. It depended on the weather conditions. If it were dry and a lot of people were in the chambers, it went comparatively fast.

Q   How long a time did the gassing take?

A   As I already stated, from three or five minutes to fifteen minutes.

Q   And how would you know when they all were dead?

A   There was an aperture, or vision slit through which one could look.

Q   And did you hear any noises from the outside?

A   Yes, but only muffled, because the walls were very thick cement, so that it was almost impossible to hear anything.

HOESS

Q   And after how long a time were the doors opened?

A   After half an hour, as in the case of the other places.

Q   And who went in to remove the bodies?

A   The detail of prisoners who were working there. I might add that in the installations of the plants electrical ventilators were added which removed the gas fumes.

Q   But was not it quite dangerous work for these inmates to go into these chambers and work among the bodies and among the gas fumes?

A   No.

Q   Did they carry gas masks?

A   They had some, but they did not need them, as nothing ever happened.

Q   Then the bodies were removed to where?

A   Into the crematorium that was situated above.

Q   Did they have elevators?

A   Yes.

113

Q   Where were the rings removed. Was it in the gas chamber itself?

A   No, there was an anti-chamber outside the gas chamber just before the elevator where the rings were removed.

Q   And where they pulled out the gold teeth?

A   Yes.

Q   How were the crematoriums arranged?

A   There were four crematoriums. The first two larger ones had five double furnaces, and they could burn two thousand human beings in twelve hours.

Q   What kind of fuel did you use?

A   Coke.

Q   And the bodies were just shoved in, were they?

A   There were little barrels as used in the crematoriums in towns and the bodies

HOESS

were pushed up to the opening and slid in.

Q   How many bodies could one oven take or hold?

A   This double furnace could take in three corpses at one time.

Q   How many minutes would it take before the body was reduced to ashes?

A   It was difficult to say. When the full burning power of this furnace
was still available, the process took place comparatively fast, but later on
after a lot of bodies had been burned, it was more slowly, but then it also
depended on the body composition of the corpse.

Q   What kind of bodies burned faster?

A   The heavy set fat persons.

Q   Did you get any fat persons, or strong persons into the ovens?

A   I do not mean strong bodies, but heavy fat persons.

Q   Were you often present at these executions and burnings?

A   Yes.

Q   Why?

A   Because I had to do this. I had to supervise these proceedings.

Q   Why did you have to supervise these proceedings?

A   To see that everything was carried out in an orderly manner.

Q   Was it interesting?

A   No, certainly not.

Q   Why not? They were enemies of German people who were executed,
weren't they?

A   But the procedure was not such that one might take an interest in.

Q   You told me yesterday that Himmler had explained to you that every
Jew irrespective of sex, or age, was a danger to the German people?

A   Yes.

Q   So it must have been quite a satisfaction for you, wasn't it, to
see that danger to the German people was removed so efficiently?

HOESS

A   No, certainly not.

Q   You reported very often in Berlin, didn't you?

A   No, never.

Q   You never left Auschwitz after the executions on a large scale started?

A   Not to report about these proceedings.

Q   What did you report in Berlin?

A   I was called for a commanders' meeting, but was called by my superior authority, and my superior officer did the questioning what they wanted to know from me, but I do not know today any more what they were.2

Q   You remember in November 1942 you were in Berlin at Eichmann's office to a meeting of experts belonging to the section organized for the solution of the Jewish question?

A   Yes.

Q   Did you give a lecture there?

A   No, not I.

Q   Didn't you explain how efficient the set-up in Auschwitz worked?

A   No.

Q   Who gave the lectures there?

A   Eichmann and various leaders from the countries of Belgium, and Hungary and so on, whatever they were.

Q   Were there maps for them to study?

A   (No answer)

Q   I do not mean in Auschwitz, but in Berlin at the meeting?

A   No.

Q   No statistical material?

A   No, the various experts of the different countries only disclosed how many Jews had already been delivered into the camps, and how many could still be expected to be delivered.

115

- 19 -

HOESS

Q   You just sat as a listener, and did not explain to the gahhering there what had happened?

A   They knew what was there.

Q   How did they know. You told me youhad been told by Himmler this was a top secret, which no one was supposed to know anything about except you.

A   Yes, that was in the year of 1941 when I received this instruction by Reichfuehrer of SS to keep it a secret, but in the meantime the various offices had received all these people, and their instructions, so that these experts should have known by now what had been going on.

Q   Can you remember any one of the gentlemen present?

A   There was Eichmann, Sturmbannfuehrer Guenther, I do not know his first name. I only know one, that was Eichmann's deputy.

Q   Who else?

116

A   I do not know the others by name. The only one that I still recall was the man from Slovakia, Wisliceny, and I believe perhaps a Dr. Seidl.

Q   What country did he represent?

A   I do not know.

Q   Was Abromeit there?

A   I do not know.

Q   Was Dannecker there?

A   Yes, Dannecker was there.

Q   Was Brunner there?

A   Yes, Brunner was there.

Q   Was Krumey there?

A   I know Krumey, but I don't know if he was there.

- 20 -

HOESS

Q   Where did you know Krumey before?

A   Krumey was in Auschwitz one time by order of Eichmann.

Q   Was Hauptsturmfuehrer Burger there?

A   I don't know him. I never heard his name.

Q   Do you know Hauptsturmfuehrer Novak?

A   Yes, he was there.

Q   What was Novak's speciality?

A   I don't know.

Q   How did you know of him?

A   I met him in the office at Eichmann's and in Guenther's office. He was in Guenther's anti-chambers.

Q   Did you have anything to do with Hrosinek?

A   I never heard of that name.

Q   Or Hartenberger?

A   No.

Q   Or Hartmann?

A   I also don't know him.

Q   How about Rudolf Jaenisch?

A   Yes, he is known to me. The name is known by me.

Q   Was he at the meeting?

A   Yes, Jaenisch was also in the outer office of Eichmann and Guenther. He was more or less an adjutant in this office.

Q   I am showing you a document marked "Appendix A 1, Position of sub section 1V A 4 b in Amt 1V of RSHA, responsible for solution of the Jewish question (Judenreferat)" and tell me if you know some of the names I have not mentioned on the bottom of the page? (Interrogator folded down lower bottom end of the document).

117

21

Q   I saw Moess and Woern; Kryshak, I don't know.

A   These two you saw at the meeting, too?

Q   I certainly know Moess, and that I saw him.

A   This is a chart of the setup of RSHA with the channels from the top down, and the sub-section for solution of the Jewish question. According to your knowledge, is this correct?

A   (Witness looks at the chart.)   It is correct.

Q   You remember you are testifying under oath, and you can now say on your oath that it is correct?

A   Yes.

Q   Now the names. RSHA Kaltenbrunner, is that correct?

A   Yes.

Q   Chief of Gestapo and Amt IV Mueller?

A   Yes, sir.

Q   Chief of Section Amt IV A 4 Eichmann?

A   Yes.

Q   Chief of sub-section for solution of Jewish Question, also Eichmann?

A   Yes.

Q   And subordinate to this sub-section of Central Department for Regulation of the Jewish question in Bohemia and Moravia?

A   Yes.

Q   That is also correct?

A   Yes.

Q   And also subordinate to sub-section IV A 4 b was the Central Agency for Jewish Emigration in Vienna?

A   Yes, that is also correct. Later on Obersturmbannfuehrer Krumey in '44 and was chief in Vienna.

Q   But this is correct, and that is, the predecessor was Haptsturm-

118

fuehrer Brunner?

A   That is correct.

Q   And his deputy was Girzick?

A   I have never heard that. I do not know that.

Q   Turning to the meeting in November 1942, what did Eichmann lecture upon?

A   It was the other way around. The various representatives of the different countries had to report on the conditions in their countries to Eichmann.

Q   But in the presence of all the participants in the meeting?

A   Yes. It was more in the manner of a round table discussion. Every participant asked Eichmann what he was to do about difficulties that had come up. For instance, in France, it was asked what was to be done about difficulties that had come up with the railroad and the Wehrmacht, and so on, and then these questions were answered.

Q   What difficulties were there in connection with the Wehrmacht?

A   Mostly it was a question of transport and the Wehrmacht control of rail transportation, that they did not always make the rolling stock available.

Q   What was Eichmann's answer to this difficulty?

A   Eichmann told them they should turn in their difficulties. That he knows them, and that he knew they might request assistance there, and, besides that, the people at the meeting had to disclose how many Jews they had already evacuated, and how many according to their estimate were still to be expected, and that was also the reason why I had to be present.

Q   Was the word "Endloesung", final solution, used at this meeting?

A   Yes, that was Eichmann's expression.

Q   What did that mean?

A   That meant extermination, as I have already explained it to you.

23

HOESS.

Q   Can you state, absolutely definitely, what did the word "Endloesung",
final solution, stand for?

A   I can only tell you what I understand by it, as I understood it from the
Reichsfuehrer.

Q   And what did it mean?

A   It meant, extermination.

Q   Of whom?

A   Of the Jews.

Q   So that the word or words "final solution" were used in this circle,
which meant biological extermination of the Jews?

A   Yes.

Q   And after this meeting, did you go back to Auschwitz?

A   Yes.

Q   What was the next meeting you attended?

A   Never attended another meeting with Eichmann.

Q   In 1943, were you in Berlin at a meeting where Eichmann explained to
the different ministries, or representatives from the different ministries, what
"Endloesung" meant?

A   No.

Q   Where he explained that "Endloesung" allegedly only meant sterilization
and evacuation of the Jews?

A   No, I do not know.

Q   Did you hear of such a meeting?

A   No, this is the first time I heard about it.

Q   Are you sure of that?

A   Yes. I only participated in one meeting with Eichmann; never at any other
time.

Q   You were never at any meeting in which representatives of the ministry

HOESS

were present?

A   No, never.

Q   Why did you go to Budapest in May 1944?

A   Because I had received a commission by my superior, Gruppenfuehrer
Gluecks, who had charged me to go there to find out how many Jews could still be
expected for the armament industries that were to be started, so they could know
how many they should count on for manpower.

Q   How did you find that out?

A   First, after I had received this commission of Gruppenfuehrer Gluecks,
I got in touch with Gruppenfuehrer Mueller in Berlin, in order to find out information from him because he was the superior authority.

Q   Just a moment. Was he the superior echelon for Gluecks?

A   No, this has nothing to do with Gluecks. He was the superior authority
for Eichmann.   121

Q   Why did you go to Mueller?

A   Because Gruppenfuehrer Mueller had to be informed by his expert, Eichmann,
how many Jews could still be expected from Hungary.

Q   How would Eichmann know that?

A   Because Eichmann was the competent man charged with this question.

Q   For what was he competent? Hungary was not Germany?

A   But Eichmann was in Hungary at that time.

Q   What did he do there?

A   He was in charge of all of the evacuation, of the entire evacuation.

Q   What evacuation?

A   The evacuation of Jews.

Q   But there were no German Jews in Hungary?
A   No Hungarian Jews.

25

HOESS

Q   How could the Germans take care of the evacuation, as you call it, of Hungarian Jews?

A   I don't know that.

Q   Is not that peculiar?

A   It happened in other countries, too.

Q   But Hungary was an Ally?

A   I don't know the Agreements that had been reached between the governments of these various countries.

Q   But you knew there were agreements between Hungary and Germany?

A   Yes, because otherwise they could not have been evacuated.

Q   Have you seen any agreement?

A   No.

Q   Did Eichmann tell you anything about agreements?

A   Yes.

Q   In the Hotel Astoria in Budapest?

A   No. I was never in any hotel in Budapest, but I was in his office on Schwabemberg in Budapest.

Q   Where did you stay in Budapest?

A   I stayed with Eichmann in his house.

Q   Let's go back to Berlin, and talk about Gruppenfuehrer Mueller, what kind of information did he give you?

A   He could not give me any information. He only told me that I should go to Budapest myself, and get in touch with Eichmann and ask him about it.

Q   So you went to Budapest?

A   Yes.

122

HOESS

Q   When was that?

A   I cannot give you the date exactly.

Q   What month?

A   It was in the Spring 1944.

Q   So when you saw Eichmann, what did he tell you?

A   He also could not give an exact figure, but that it was estimated about two million Jews were present in Hungary.

Q   And all two million were to be sent to Auschwitz?

A   He said right away this estimate in his opinion was too high. He did not know how many there were, but that he believed that number was too much.

Q   Did he feel sorry he could not get two million?

A   No, he merely said that was not correct.

Q   How many did he expect to get from Hungary?

A   Half a million.

123

Q   All for labor purposes?

A   No, Eichmann had nothing to do with selecting those who were fit for labor. His office took no interest in this question at all.

Q   They only had the interest of getting them exterminated, hadn't they?

A   Yes.

Q   So Eichmann could not give you any figures. Who gave you the figures?

A   Nobody could give me any information.

Q   Who was present at that discussion with Eichmann in his office?

A   So far as I know they were Eichmann, Hunsche and Brunner.

Q   And Wisliceny?

A   I met him later in Mungatz.

27

Q   During your discussion with Eichmann in his office in Budapest, did you discuss the percentage of Jews who possibly could be used for labor?

A   Yes, that was the very reason for my trip.

Q   How many persons did you estimate could be used from Hungary, of the Jews, for purposes other than gassing?

A   I didn't know that at the time. I only found that out later.

Q   I am not talking about the number of Jews you were going to get for labor, or other purposes. I am talking about the percentage?

A   I cannot get any picture of that.

Q   But, you had an experience second to no other in the whole world, as to the percentage of Jews who could be used for labor. You had viewed Jews arriving in Auschwitz for years, and yesterday you mentioned a percentage between twenty to thirty percent were useful, is that right?

124   A   Yes, but I did also mention that it was different for each country.

Q   But you hoped, didn't you, that you would be able to get around twenty to twenty five percent for labor?

A   I hoped even more than that.   I hoped that in Hungary we should be able to use at least thirty-five percent for labor purposes.

Q   Did you mention that to Eichmann?

A   Yes.

Q   How did he like it?

A   He said that he could not form an opinion, because he had not seen them, so he could not make any estimate.

Q   What was your reason to believe that thirty-five percent of the Hungarian Jews could be used for labor?

A   Because for a large part, the Jews there were people from the farms, and from the agriculture districts.

HOESS

Q   So you were unable to get any definite information in Eichmann's office,
then you decided to take a little trip around to the concentration camps to look at
the Jews, didn't you?

A   Yes.

Q   Then you went first of all to Mungatz?

A   Yes.

Q   Who was in charge there?

A   Wisliceny.

Q   Why was he there?

A   He was in charge for the total area of Mungatz, that is to say, Section
No. 1.

Q   How was it that the German SS Hauptsturmfuehrer was in charge of the
collecting of Hungarian Jews?

A   No, that is not correct. The actual collecting and imprisonment of
these Hungarian Jews was carried out by the Hungarian police and Gendarmerie.

Q   And what was Wisliceny's job there?

A   So far as I could find out he was commissioned by Eichmann to determine
that the collection and the gathering of the Jews were carried out in proper manner.

Q   What is a proper manner?

A   Proper manner was perhaps of two functions, to see that the Hungarian
police stayed to the agreements that had been reached between the various governments,
but I do not know what agreements they were and that all the Jews were collected.

Q   Did he have a Hungarian opposite number? Was his name Ferenscy?

A   Ferenscy is the name I heard in Budapest. He was a Chief of the Hungarian
Field Gendarmerie, but I do not know the name of Wisliceny's opposite number.

125

HOESS

Q   How long did you stay in Mungatz?

A   One day.

Q   What did you do there?

A   I went out to the brickyards where the Jews had been collected, and
took about one-thousand Jews at random, and with the help of a Jewish docotr, who
had been given the job by a Hungarian officer from the Field Gendarmerie, selected
those people whom he considered fit for labor, or in order to get an idea.

Q   How many were fit for labor?

A   About thirty percent in Mungatz, but there were many brickyard/in
Mungatz, and in the vicinity of Mungatz, about thirty.

Q   So you went from one camp to another?

A   Yes.

Q   And the average was about thirty percent?

A   Yes, the average for the area of Mundatz was about thirty percent.

Q   And this was Sector 1?

A   Yes. I am not quite sure that I can state definitely whether this
sector was called Sector 1, or Sector 1V. It was the area "Karpatho-Ukraine."

Q   And then you travelled from sector to sector, and made your investigation

A   No, I only travelled to the south in the neighborhood of the Danube
River. That was another sector. I didn't know whether No. 1, or No. 1V, but it
was in the southern sector, and there Dannecker was in charge.

Q   And what was the qualify of the Jews there?

A   It was less good, because there were more city people there.

Q   Then you returned to Budapest?

A   Yes.

Q   And reported to whom?

30

HOESS

A   Again to Eichmann's office, and then I returned immediately to Berlin.

Q   Did you see Mueller?

A   No, I did not go there.

Q   Did you see any well known faces in Budapest while you were outside your narrow circle of collaborators?

A   I only went, together with Eichmann, to the Obergruppenfuehrer Winkelmann higher SS and Police Leader, because I had to report to him anyhow.

Q   Did you meet Kaltenbrunner there?

A   No.

Q   Did you hear that Kaltenbrunner was in Budapest?

A   No, not when I was there.

MR. JAARI: We will finish now and continue the hearing later on.

-o-o-o-o-o-o-o-o-o-o-o-o-o-o-   127

APPROVED:

_____
                INTERROGATOR

_____
                INTERPRETER

_____
                COURT REPORTER.

31

                                        HOESS.

Doc. 4

128

TAKEN FROM DACHAU GAS
INSTALLATION — 4/7/46
by before H. Booth, H.S. Ci
+ others

Labels on Poison Gas Cans
Taken from Dachau Poison Gas Installations on 7 April 1946 by Alfred H. Booth, U.S. Civilian, X-04625H.

Durability guaranteed only for a period of three months' storage time with consumer!

ZYKLON

Tesch & Stabenow
International Insecticide Co., Ltd.
HAMBURG 1 - MESSBERGHOF
Authorized for use in the territory of
the Reich east of the Elbe, the
Sudetengau, the General Government, the
Reich Commissariat Ostland, and
Denmark, Finland, and Norway.

POISON GAS!

D.R.P. 575293
CYANIDE PREPARATION!
To be stored in cool
and dry places. To
be kept safe from
sun and open flames.

D.R.P. 575293
To be opened
and used only
by trained
personnel.

ZYKLON

DEGESCH

ZYKLON

Contains 200g of Cyanide

A PRODUCT OF THE GERMAN INSECTICIDE CO.,
LTD.
FRANKFURT o/MAIN

Durability guaranteed only for a period of three months' storage time with consumer!

DEGESCH

ZYKLON

Contains 200g of Cyanide

GERMAN INSECTICIDE CO., LTD.
FRANKFURT o/MAIN

POISON GAS!

D.R.P. 575293
CYANIDE PREPARATION!
To be stored in cool
and dry places. To
be kept safe from
sun and open flames.

D.R.P. 575293
To be opened
and used only
by trained
personnel.

ZYKLON

DEGESCH

ZYKLON

Contains 200g of Cyanide

GERMAN INSECTICIDE CO., LTD.
FRANKFURT o/MAIN

129

CERTIFICATE OF TRANSLATION
OF DOCUMENT NI-032
----

15 May 1946

I, Alfred H. Booth U.S. Civilian AGO No. X-046254 hereby certify that I am thoroughly conversant with the English and German languages; and that the above is a true and correct translation of Document NI-032.

ALFRED H. BOOTH
U.S. CIVILIAN
AGO NO. 046254

130

STAFF EVIDENCE ANALYSIS   By: A.H.Elbau
                                           Date: 21 August 1947

Document no.   NI-9912

Title and/ or general nature: Directions for the use of prussic
                                    acid (Zyklon).

Date:

Sonrce (Location of original, etc.):

                                    Source: File "Zyklon-Versand",
                                    DEGESCH, Schaumainkai 43,
                                    Frankfurt/Main
                                    Location: Document Control Branch,
                                    OCCWC, Nuernberg, Germany

Doc. 5

PERSONS, FIRMS OR ORGANIZATIONS INVOLVED: **131**

                                    NI- IG Farben
                                    NI- IGF DEGESCH
                                    NI- IGF Poison Gas
                                    NI- IGF Atrocities

TO BE FILED UNDER THESE REFERENCE HEADINGS:

                                    See above

SUMMARY (Indicate page numbers):

P.1: "Zyklon is the absorption of a mixture of prussic acid and an irritant
by a base material (Traegerstoff).... The irritant has besides his function
as warning agent the advantage that it stimulates the breathing of insects."

End

NI-9912

Richtlinien für die Anwendung von Blausäure (Zyklon) zur Ungeziefervertilgung (Entwesung).

I. Eigenschaften der Blausäure.

Blausäure ist ein Gas, das sich durch Verdunsten entwickelt.

Siedepunkt: 26° C.

Gefrierpunkt: — 15° C.

Spez. Gewicht: 0.69.

Dampfdichte: 0.97 (Luft = 1.0).

Flüßigkeit ist leicht verdampfbar.

Flüßigkeit: wasserhell, farblos.

Geruch: eigenartig, widerlich süßlich.

Außerordentlich großes Durchdringungsvermögen.

Blausäure ist im Wasser löslich.

Explosionsgefahr: 75 g Blausäure auf 1 cbm Luft. (Normale Anwendung ca 8—10 g pro cbm, daher nicht explosiv). Blausäure darf nicht mit offenem Feuer, glühenden Drähten usw. zusammengebracht werden. Sie verbrennt dann langsam und verliert vollkommen ihre Wirkung. (Es entsteht Kohlensäure, Wasser und Stickstoff.)

Giftigkeit für Warmblüter.

Blausäure hat fast keine Warnwirkung, daher ist sie hochgiftig und hochgefährlich. Blausäure gehört zu den stärksten Giften. 1 mg pro kg — Körpergewicht genügt, um einen Menschen zu töten. Kinder und Frauen sind im allgemeinen empfindlicher als Männer. Ganz geringe Mengen von Blausäure schaden dem Menschen nicht, auch bei stetiger Atmung. Vögel und Fische sind besonders empfindlich gegen Blausäure.

Giftigkeit für Insekten.

Die Wirkung der Blausäure auf Insekten hängt nicht so sehr von der Temperatur ab, wie die Wirkung anderer Gase; d. h. sie wirkt auch bei kalten Temperaturen (auch noch bei — 5° C). Bei vielen Tieren, besonders bei Wanzen und Läusen, sind die Eier empfindlicher, als die Imagines.

Giftigkeit gegen Pflanzen:

Der Grad der Giftwirkung hängt ab von dem Vegetationszustand der Pflanzen. Hartlaubige Pflanzen sind weniger empfindlich als weichlaubige. Schimmelpilze und Hausschwamm werden durch Blausäure nicht abgetötet.

Bakterien werden durch Blausäure nicht vernichtet.

II. Anwendungsform der Blausäure.

Zyklon
ist die Aufsaugung eines Gemisches von Blausäure und Reizstoff in einem Trägerstoff. Als Trägerstoff verwendet man entweder Holzfaserscheiben, eine rotbraunekörnige Masse (Diagrieß) oder kleine blaue Würfel (Erco).

Der Reizstoff hat außer seinem Zweck als Warnstoff noch den Vorteil, daß er die Atmung der Insekten anregt. Entwicklung der Blausäure und des Reizstoffes durch einfache Verdunstung. Haltbarkeit des Zyklons 3 Monate. Schadhafte Dosen zuerst verbrauchen. Inhalt einer Dose muß stets ganz verbraucht werden. Flüßige Blausäure greift Polituren, Lacke, Farben usw. an. Gasförmige Blausäure ist unschädlich. Durch den Reizstoffzusatz bleibt die Giftigkeit der Blausäure unverändert; die Gefährlichkeit ist aber wesentlich geringer geworden.

Zyklon kann durch Verbrennen unschädlich gemacht werden.

III. Vergiftungsmöglichkeiten:

1. Leichte Vergiftungen:

Schwindelgefühl, Kopfschmerzen, Erbrechen, Unwohlsein usw. Alle diese Anzeichen gehen vorüber, wenn man sofort in die frische Luft geht. Alkohol setzt die Widerstandsfähigkeit bei Blausäuredurchgasungen herab. Daher vor der Vergasung keinen Alkohol trinken.

Man gibt: 1 Tablette Cardiazol oder Veriazol, um Herzstörungen vorzubeugen, gegebenenfalls nach 2 bis 3 Stunden nochmals.

2. Schwere Vergiftungen:

Der Betroffene fällt plötzlich zusammen und ist bewustlos. Erste Hilfe: Frische Luft, Gasmaske ab, Kleidung lockern, künstliche Atmung. Lobelin i. m. 0,01 g. Kampfer-Injektionen sind verboten.

132

3. Vergiftungen durch die Haut:

Anzeichen wie unter 1. Desgleichen auch Behandlung.

4. Magenvergiftungen:

sind zu behandeln mit:

Lobelin, 0.01 g i. m.,
Eisenvitriol.
gebrannte Magnesia.

IV. Gasschutz.

Bei Durchgasungen mit Zyklon nur Spezialfilter. z. B. Filtereinsatz »J« (blaubraun) der Auergesellschaft. Berlin, oder der Drägerwerke, Lübeck, verwenden.

Tritt Gas durch die Maske, unverzüglich das Gebäude verlassen und Filter wechseln, nachdem auch die Maske und der Maskensitz auf Dichtigkeit geprüft sind. Der Filtereinsatz ist erschöpft. wenn Gas durch die Maske tritt. Mit Filter »J« erst ca 2 Minuten im Freiem bewegen. damit eine gewisse Feuchtigkeit durch die Ausatemluft im Filtereinsatz erreicht wird. — Filter darf keinesfalls im gaserfüllten Raum gewechselt werden.

V. Personal:

Für jede Entwesung wird ein Entwesungstrup eingesetzt bestehend aus mindestens 2 Mann. — Verantwortlich für die Durchgasung ist der Durchgasungsleiter. Ihm obliegt besonders die Besichtigung. Lüftung, Freigabe und die Sicherheitsmaßnahmen. Für den Fall seines Ausscheidens bestimmt der Durchgasungsleiter einen Stellvertreter. Den Anordnungen des Durchgasungsleiters ist unverzüglich nachzukommen.

Unausgebildete Personen oder ausgebildede, die noch keine Bescheinigung besitzen, dürfen nicht zu Gasarbeiten herangezogen werden. Sie dürfen auch nicht in gaserfüllte Räume hinein genommen werden. Der Durchgasungsleiter muß stets wissen, wo seine Leute zu erreichen sind. Sämtliche Leute müssen sich jederzeit darüber ausweisen können, daß sie die behördliche. Genehmigung besitzen, Blausäure zur Schädlingsbekämpfung zu verwenden.

Die vorliegenden Richtlinien sind in allen Fällen genau zu beachten.

VI. Ausrüstung:

Jeder muß stets bei sich führen:

1. Seine eigene Gasmaske.
2. Mindestens 2 Spezial-Einsätze gegen Zyklon-Blausäure.
3. Das Merkblatt: »Erste Hilfe bei Blausäurevergifteten«.
4. Arbeitsvorschrift.
5. Zulassungsbescheinigung.

Jeder Entwesungstrupp hat stets bei sich zu führen:

1. Mindestens 3 Spezial-Einsätze als weiteren Vorrat.
2. 1 Gasrestnachweisgerät.
3. 1 Vorrichtung. um Lobelin einzuspritzen.
4. Lobelin 0.01 g Ampullen.
5. (Cardiazol). Veriazol Tabletten.
6. 1 Hebelöffner oder Spitzhammer zum Öffnen der Zyklondosen.
7. Warnungsschilder der vorgeschriebenen Art.
8. Abdichtungsmittel.
9. Papierbogen zur Unterlage.
10. Elektr. Taschenlampe.

Alle Geräte sind stets sauber und in Ordnung zu halten. Beschädigungen von Geräten sind sofort auszubessern.

VII. Planung einer Durchgasung:

1. Ist die Durchgasung überhaupt durchführbar?
   a) Bauart und Lage des Gebäudes.
   b) Beschaffenheit des Daches.
   c) Beschaffenheit der Fenster.
   d) Vorhandensein von Heizkanälen, Luftschächten, Mauerdurchbrüchen usw.
2. Feststellung der Art der zu vertilgenden Schädlinge.
3. Raumberechnung.
   (Nicht auf Pläne verlassen, sondern selbst ausmessen. Nur Außenmaße nehmen. Mauerwerk mitberechnen.)
4. Vorbereitung der Belegschaft.
   (Entfernung von Nutztieren, Pflanzen, Nahrungsmittel, unentwickelte fotografische Platten, Genußmittel, Gasmaskenfilter).
5. Feststellung besonders schwieriger Abdichtungen.
   (Luftschächte, Kanäle, Holzverschalungen für große Öffnungen, Dächer.)
6. Feststellung der zu treffenden Sicherheitsmaßnahmen.
   (Bewachung, Arbeitskommando zum Verkleben.)
7. Festsetzung des Durchgasungstages und der Räumungsfrist.
8. Gegebenen Falles Sicherheitsmaßnahmen für die Nachbarschaft rechtzeitig veranlassen.
9. Anmeldung bei der Behörde.

VIII. Vorbereitung einer Durchgasung:

1. Abdichtung.
2. Öffnen sämtlicher Türen. Schränke, Schubladen usw.
3. Betten auseinanderlegen.
4. Entfernung offener Flüssigkeit (Kaffeereste, Waschwasser usw.).

133

5. Entfernung von Lebensmitteln.
6. Entfernung von Pflanzen und Nutztieren (Aquarien usw.).
7. Entfernung unentwickelter fotogr. Platten und Filme.
8. Entfernen von Verbandspflaster, Arzneimitteln offen und in Tüten (besonders Kohle).
9. Entfernung von Gasmaskenfiltern.
10. Vorbereitung der Erfolgsprüfung.
11. Räumung von der Belegschaft.
12. Schlüsselübernahme. (Sämtliche Türenschlüssel.)

IX. Gasstärke und Einwirkungszeit hängen ab von der Art der Schädlinge, der Temperatur, dem Füllungsgrad der Räume und der Dichtigkeit des Gebäudes.

Bei Innentemperaturen von über + 5° C nimmt man in der Regel 8 g/cbm Blausäure.

Einwirkungszeit 16 Stunden, wenn nicht besondere Verhältnisse, z. B. geschlossene Bauweise, eine Verkürzung erfordern. Bei warmem Wetter darf man bis auf 6 Stunden heruntergehen. Bei Temperaturen von unter + 5° C ist die Einwirkungszeit auf mindestens 32 Stunden zu verlängern.

Die angegebene Stärke und E.-Zeit ist anzuwenden bei: Wanzen, Läusen, Flöhen usw. mit Eiern, Larven und Puppen.

Bei Kleidermotten über plus 10° C 16 g/cbm und 24 Std. Einw.-Zeit. Mehlmotten wie Wanzen.

X. Durchgasung eines Gebäudes:
1. Prüfung, ob das Gebäude von allen Menschen verlassen ist.
2. Auspacken der Zyklonkisten. Für jeden Stockwerk die entsprechende Menge bereitstellen.
3. Verteilung der Dosen. Ein Mann begibt sich in das Gebäude, empfängt dort die die vom Arbeitskommando heraufgebrachten Dosen und verteilt sie. (Läßt sie neben die Unterlagebogen stellen.)
4. Entlassung des Arbeitskommandos.
5. Aufstellung der Wache und Belehrung dieser durch den Durchgasungsleiter.
6. Überprüfung der völligen Abdichtung und Räumung.
7. Anlegung des Gasschutzes.
8. Öffnen der Dosen und Ausschütten des Doseninhaltes. Der Inhalt ist dünn auszustreuen, damit das Zyklon schnell verdunstet und möglichst schnell die notwendige Gasstärke erreicht wird. Die Beschickung beginnt im obersten Stockwerk. der Keller wird vor dem Erdgeschoß beschickt. fals ersteres keinen Ausgang hat. Bereits beschickte Räume sollen nach Möglichkeit nicht noch einmal betreten

werden. Bei der Beschickung ist ruhig und langsam zu arbeiten. Besonders ist die Treppe langsam zu begehen. Die Beschickung darf nur im Notfalle unterbrochen werden.
9. Die Ausgangstüre wird verschlossen, abgedichtet (Schlüsselloch nicht vergessen) und der Schlüssel dem Durchgasungsleiter übergeben.
10. Auf die Tür wird eine Warnungstaffel aufgeklebt mit der Aufschrift: »Vorsicht, giftige Gase. Lebensgefahr. Eintritt verboten.« Die Warnungstafel muß — falls erforderlich — mehrsprachig sein. Jedenfalls muß sie mindestens 1 deutlich sichtbaren Totenkopf tragen.
11. Gasschutz, Einrichtungen zur Wiederbelebung und Gasrestnachweis sind bereit zu halten. Jedermann des Durchgasungspersonals muß wissen, wo sich die Gegenstände befinden.
12. Mindestens 1 Mann des Durchgasungspersonals bleibt stets in erreichbarer Nähe des unter Gas stehenden Gebäudes. Sein Aufenthaltsort ist der Wache bekannt zu geben.

XI. Lüftung:

Die Lüftung bietet die größte Gefahr für Beteiligte und Unbeteiligte. Sie ist deshalb besonders vorsichtig und stets mit angelegter Gasmaske auszuführen. Grundsätzlich soll derart gelüftet werden, daß gasfreie Luft stets in kürzester Zeit erreichbar ist, daß d. Gas nach einer Seite abzieht, auf der die Gefährdung Unbeteiligter ausgeschlossen ist. Bei schwieriger Lüftung bleibt 1 ausgebildeter Mann vor dem Gebäude, um den Abzug des Gases zu beobachten.

1. Dafür sorgen, daß sich in der Umgebung des Gebäudes keine fremden Leute aufhalten.
2. Die Wachposten so aufstellen, daß sie durch das abziehende Gas nicht belästigt werden. trotzdem aber die Zugänge zu dem Gebäude beobachten können.
3. Gasmaske anlegen.
4. Gebäude betreten. Türe schließen, nicht verschließen.
5. Zuerst die Fenster auf der dem Wind abgekehrten Seite des Gebäudes öffnen. Stockwerkweise lüften. Im Erdgeschoß beginnen und nach jedem Stockwerk eine Erholungspause von mindestens 10 Minuten einlegen.
6. In den einzelnen Räumen des Gebäudes müssen die Türen zum Gang. Verbindungstüren zwischen den Zimmern und die Fenster geöffnet werden. Bieten einige Fenster Schwierigkeiten. so dürfen sie erst geöffnet werden. wenn die Hauptmenge des Gases abgezogen ist.

134

7. Verschläge und andere nicht leicht wieder herstellbare Abdichtungen dürfen erst entfernt werden, wenn die Hauptmenge des Gases abgezogen ist.

8. Bei Frost und Frostgefahr ist darauf zu achten, daß Heizung und Wasserleitung nicht einfrieren.

9. Zimmer mit wertvollen Inhalt wie Kleiderkammern usw., dürfen wieder verschlossen werden, sobald die Fenster geöffnet sind.

10. Geöffnete Fenster und Türen sind gegen Zuschlagen zu sichern.

11. Abdichtungen der Schornsteine werden nach der vorläufigen Freigabe entfernt.

12. Die Lüftung muß mindestens 20 Std. dauern.

13. Die Wache bleibt während der ganzen Lüftungszeit bei dem Gebäude.

II. Vorläufige Freigabe:

Ein durchgaster Raum darf vorläufig freigegeben werden, sobald bei offenem Fenster und Tür der Papierstreifen des Gasrestnachweises schwächer blau, als das mittlere Farbmuster ist. In vorläufig freigegebenen Räumen dürfen nur Arbeiten zur Lüftung und Aufräumung ausgeführt werden. Keinesfalls darf in ihnen ausgeruht oder, geschlafen weerden. Fenster und Türen müssen ständig geöffnet bleiben.

XIII. Aufräumungsarbeiten nach der vorläufigen Freigabe:

1. Entfernung der Zyklonrückstände aus den durchgasten Räumen. Sie sind im allgemeinen wie Dosen und Kisten an die Fabrik zurückzusenden. Vor der Rücksendung aus den durchgasten Räume muß auf den Kisten die Aufschrift »Gift« entfernt werden. Feuchte, nasse oder verschmutzte Rückstände, sowie beschädigte Dosen, dürfen keinesfalls zurückgesandt werden. Sie können auf den Kehricht oder Schlakkenhaufen geworfen worden, dürfen jedoch niemals in Wasserläufe entleert werden.

2. Matratzen, Strohsäcke, Kissen, Polstermöbel oder ähnliche Gegenstände sind unter Aufsicht des Durchgasungsleiters oder seines Beauftragten mindestens eine Stunde lang im Freiem (bei Regenwetter mindestens 2 Std. auf der Flur) zu schütteln oder zu klopfen.

3. Wenn es möglich ist, soll die Füllung der Strohsäcke erneuert werden. Die alte Fül-

lung darf aber nicht verbrannt, sondern kann nach weiterer Lüftung wieder verwendet werden.

4. Falls die Schornsteine oben abgedeckt worden sind, müssen die Abdichtungen sorgfältig entfernt werden, andersfalls Gefahr besteht, daß das Feuer in Öfen und Herden keinen genügenden Zug hat und Kohlenoxydvergiftungen hervorgerufen werden.

5. Nach der endgültigen Freigabe ist ein Durchgasungsbericht nach vorgeschriebenen Muster in doppelter Ausfertigung auszufüllen. Aus ihm müssen insbesondere zu ersehen sein:

   a) durchgaster Rauminhalt,
   b) Menge des verbrauchten Zyklons,
   c) Name des Durchgasungsleiters,
   d) Namen des übrigen Personalstandes,
   e) Gaseinwirkungszeit;
   f) Zeitpunkt der Freigabe der entwesten Räume.

XIV. Endgültige Freigabe:

1. Keinesfalls vor Ablauf von 21 Stunden nach Beginn der Lüftung.

2. Alle zum Ausklopfen herausgebrachten Gegenstände sind in den Raum zurückzubringen.

3. Fenster und Türen werden für eine Stunde geschlossen.

4. In heizbaren Räumen muß eine Temperatur von mindestens 15° C hergestellt werden.

5. Gasrestnachweis. Der Papierstreifen darf auch zwischen übereinander gelegten Decken, Matratzen und in schwer zugänglichen und schwer lüftbaren Räumen nicht stärker blau sein, als das hellste Farbmuster. Ist dies nicht der Fall, so muß die Lüftung fortgesetzt werden und der Gasrestnachweis nach einigen Stunden wiederholt werden.

6. In Gebäuden, die möglichst bald wieder zum Schlafen benutzt werden sollen, ist der Gasrestnachweis in jedem einzelnen Raum vorzunehmen. Keinesfalls darf in einem durchgasten Raum in der auf die Durchgasung folgenden Nacht geschlafen werden. Stets müssen die Fenster in der ersten Nacht, in der der Raum wieder benutzt wird, geöffnet bleiben.

7. Der Durchgasungsleiter oder sein Stellvertreter darf das Gebäude nicht eher verlassen, als bis auch der letzte Raum endgültig freigegeben ist.

135

Herausgegeben von der Gesundheitsanstalt des Protektorates Böhmen und Mähren in Prag.

DIRECTIVES FOR THE USE OF PRUSSIC ACID (ZYKLON)

FOR THE DESTRUCTION OF VERMIN (DISINFESTATION).

1. Properties of prussic acid. (hydrocyanic acid)

Prussic acid is a gas which is generated by evaporation.

Boiling point: 25 degree Centigrade.

Freezing point: - 15 degrees Cent.

Specific gravity: 0.69

Steam density: 0.97. (Air: 1.0)

The liquid evaporates easily.

Liquid: transparent, colourless.

Smell: peculiar, repulsively sweet.

Extraordinarily great penetrative powers.

Prussic acid is soluble in water.

Danger of explosion. 75 g prussic acid 1 cbm air. (Normal application approx. 8-10 g per cbm, therefore not explosive). Prussic acid may not be brought into contact with an open flame, glowing wires etc., because then it burns up slowly and loses all its effectiveness. (carbonic acid, water and nitrogen are formed).

Toxic effects on warm-blooded animals.

Since prussic acid has practically no indicative irritant effect it is highly toxic and very dangerous. Prussic acid is one of the most powerful poisons. 1 mg per kg of body weight is sufficient to kill a human being. Women and children are generally more susceptible than men. Very small amounts of prussic acid do not harm the human body, even if breathed continously. Birds and fishes are particularly susceptible to prussic acid.

Toxic effects on insects.

The effects of prussic acid on insects do not depend on the temperature to the same extent as that of other gases,

136

1

that is, it is also effective in low temperatures (even at
5 degrees ^{C}ent.) The eggs of many insects, particularly of
bugs and lice, are more susceptible than the full-grown
insects.

Toxic effects on plants.

The degree of toxicity depends on the type of vegetation
on the plants. Plants with thick leaves are less susceptible
than those with thin ones. Mildew and dry-rot are not
killed by prussic acid. Prussic acid does not destroy bacteria.

II. Method of using prussic acid.

ZYKLON is the absorption of a mixture of prussic acid and an
irritant by a carrier. Wood fibre discs, a reddish brown
granular mass (Diagriess - Dia gravel) or small blue cubes
(^{E}rco) are used as carriers.

Apart from serving its purpose as indicator, this
irritant also has the advantage of stimulating the respiration
of insects. Prussic acid and the irritant are generated
through simple evaporation. Zyklon will keep for 3 months.
Use damaged cans first. The contents of a can must all be
used up at once. Liquid prussic acid damages polish, laquer,
paint etc. Gaseous prussic acid is harmless. ^{T}he toxicity
of the prussic acid remains unchanged by the addition of the
irritant; the danger connected with it is however
considerably decreased.

Zyklon can be rendered by combustion.

III. Possible poisoning.

    1. Slight poisoning:

Dizziness, headache, vomiting, general feeling of
sickness, etc. All these symptoms pass if one immediately
gets out into the fresh air. Alcohol reduces resistance to
prussic acid gassing, therefore do not drink alcohol before

137

2

fumigation.

Prescribe: 1 tablet Cardiazol or Veriazol in order to prevent heart disorders, if necessary repeat after 2-3 hours.

2. Severe poisoning.

The affected person will collapse suddenly and faint. First Aid: fresh air, remove gas mask, loosen clothing, apply artificial respiration. Lobelin, intermuscular 0.01g. Do not give camphor injections.

(page 2 of original)

3. Poisoning through the skin.

Symptoms as for 1. Treat in the same way.

4. Stomach poisoning.

Treat with

Lobelin intermuscular 0.01g.

ferrous sulphate

burnt magnesia,

IV. <u>Protection against gas.</u>

When fumigation with Zyklon use only special filters, e.g. the filter insert "J" (blue-brown) of the Auergesell-schaft Berlin or of the Draegerwerke, Luebeck. Should gas seep through the mask, leave the building immediately and change filters after also checking the mask and its fit to see whether they are tight. The filter insert is exhausted if gas enters through the mask. If using filter 'J', first move around in the open air for approx. 2 minutes so that a certain amount of moisture from the breath may gather in the filter insert. Under no circumstances should filters be changed inside gas-filled rooms.

V. <u>Personnel.</u>

A disinfestation squad consisting of at least 2 members is employed for each disinfestation project. The fumigation

138

3

chief is responsible for the fumigation. His particular

duties are inspection, airing, release and safety measures.

The fumigation chief is to appoint a deputy in case he has

to leave. The orders of the fumigation chief are to be

followed without delay.

Untrained persons or persons who are trained but who

do not yet hold a certificate may not be called in to work

on gassing operations, nor may they be taken into gas-filled

rooms. The fumigation chief must also know where to contact

his personnel. Every person must at all times be able to

prove that he has official authorization for the use of

prussic acid for extermination purposes.

VI. Equipment.

Each member must at all times carry with him:

1. His own gas mask.

2. At least 2 special filter inserts against Zyklon

prussic acid.

3. The leaflet "First Aid for prussic acid poisoning."

4. Work order.

5. Authorization certificate.

Each disinfestation squad must at all times carry:

1. At least 3 special inserts as extra stock.

2. 1 gas detector.

3. 1 instrument for injecting Lobelin.

4. Lobelin 0.01g. ampulles.

5. Cardiazol, Veriazol tablets.

6. 1 lever or pickhammer for opening the cans of Zyklon.

7. Warning signs as per regulation.

8. Material for sealing.

9. Sheets of paper to serve as pads.

10. Flashlight.

139

4

All equipment is to be kept clean and in good order at all times. Damage to equipment is to be repaired at once.

VII. Planning fumigations.

1. Can the fumigation be carried out at all?

    a) Type of building and situation.

    b) Condition of roof.

    c) Condition of windows.

    d) Presence of heating shafts, air shafts, breaks in the walls etc.

2. Determine the kind of vermin to be exterminated.

3. Calculate the space. (do not rely on drawings but take measurements yourself. Take only outside measurements, include walls)

4. Prepare personnel.

    (Remove domestic animals, plants, food and drink, undeveloped photographic plates, and gas mask filters.)

5. Find which opening will be particularly difficult to seal. (Air shafts, drains, large openings which have been boarded up, roofs.)

6. Settle necessary safety measures.

    (Guarding, work detachment for sealing)

7. Fix the date for the fumigation and the time for clearing the building.

8. If necessary, arrange safety measures for the neighborhood in good time.

9. Notify authorities.

VIII. Preparation for fumigation:

1. Seal.

2. Open all doors, closets, drawers, etc.

3. Pull bedding apart.

4. Remove all liquids (remains of coffee, washing water etc.)

140

(page 3 of original)

5. Remove all food.

6. Remove all plants and domestic animals (aquaria etc.)

7. Remove all undeveloped photographic plates and films.

8. Remove adhesive plaster, all medical supplies, whether open or in paper bags (particularly coal).

9. Remove all gas mask filters.

10. Prepare for check on results.

11. Clear out personnel.

12. Take over keys (every door key.)

IX. The strength of the gas and time required for it to take effect depend on

the type of vermin

the temperature

the amount of furniture in the rooms

the imperviousness of the building

For inside temperatures of more than 5 degrees Cent. it is customary to use 8 g prussic acid per cbm.

Time needed to take effect: 16 hours, unless there are special circumstances such as a closed-in type of building, which requires less time. If the weather is warm it is possible to reduce this to a minimum of 6 hours. The period is to be extended to at least 32 hours if the temperature is below 5 deg. Cent.

The strength and time as above are to be applied in the case of: bugs, lice, fleas etc., with eggs, larves and chrysales.

For clothes-moths: temperatures above 10 deg. Cent. 16 g per cbm and 24 hours to take effect.

For flour-moths: same as for bugs.

X. Fumigation of a building.

141

1. Check that everybody has left the building.

2. Unpack the boxes of Zyklon. Make the appropriate amount ready for each floor.

3. Distribute the cans. One man to go into the building and receive the cans which have been brought up by the work detachment and to distribute them. (Have them put next to the pads.)

4. Dismiss the work detachment.

5. Post the guard. Fumigation chief to instruct guard.

6. Check that sealing and clearing have been completed.

7. Put on gas masks.

8. Open the cans and pour out their contents. The contents are to be spread thinly so that the Zyklon can evaporate quickly and the necessary density of the gas can be achieved as soon as possible. This process is to start on the top floor but the cellar is to be dealt with before the ground floor, should the cellar have no exit. Rooms which have been dealt with should as far as possible not be re-entered. The processing is to be done slowly and calmly. The staircase particularly should only be used slowly. The processing may only be interrupted in an emergency.

9. The exit door to be locked, sealed and its key handed over to the fumigation chief.

10. On the door fix a warning sign with the legend "Danger-Poison gas. Danger to life, no admittance." This warning sign is to be in several languages if necessary, and in any case it must be marked with at least one death's head, clearly visible.

11. Gas masks, apparatus for resusitation and gas detectors are to be kept available at all times. Every member of the fumigation squad must know where these objects are located.

142

7

12. At least one member of the fumigation squad must always remain near the building which is being fumigated. The guard must be notified of his position.

XI. Airing.

The airing is connected with the greatest danger for those participating and others. Therefore it must be carried out particularly carefully and a gas mask should always be worn. The airing should place according to the following principles: pure air should always be within reach in the shortest possible time and the gas should flow out to that side where it cannot endanger people who are not participating. Should the airing be difficult one trained man should remain in front of the building in order to watch how the gas is blowing away.

1. Take care to see that no strangers remain in the vicinity of the building.

2. Post the guards in such a way that they are not annoyed by the gas as it blows out, but can still watch the entrances to the building.

3. Put on gas mask.

4. Enter building. Close door, but do not lock it.

5. First open the windows on that side of the building where there is no wind. Air floor by floor. Start on the ground floor and after each floor take at least 10 minutes' rest.

6. The doors leading to the corridor, connecting doors between rooms and windows must be opened in each room. Should there be difficulty in opening any of the windows they should only be opened after most of the gas has blown away.

(page 4 of original)

143

8

7. Partitions and other methods used to seal the room which cannot be replaced quickly should only be removed after most of the gas has blown away.

8. Care should be taken to see that the heating system and water pipes do not freeze should there be frost or danger of it.

9. Rooms with valuable contents, such as clothing stores etc. may be locked again after the windows have been opened.

10. Windows and doors which have been opened should be fastened in such a way that they cannot slam.

11. Covers in chimneys may be removed after the provisional release of the building.

12. The airing should continue for at least 20 hours.

13. The guard should remain near the building during the whole of this time.

XII. Provisional release.

A fumigated room may be released provisionally as soon as the paper strip of the gas detector is of a lighter blue than the centre colour pattern, when the doors and windows are open. Only work concerned with airing and clearing up may be done in the rooms which have been provisionally released. Under no circumstances may anyone rest or sleep in these rooms. The doors and windows must be left open all the time.

XIII. Clearing up after provisional release.-

1. Remove remains of Zyklon from the fumigated rooms. They should generally be sent back to the factory in the same way as cans and boxes. Before boxes are sent back from the fumigated rooms the inscription "Poison" must be removed from them. Damp, wet or soiled remains as well as damaged cans may not be sent back under any circumstances.

144

9

They may be thrown on a rubbish or slag heap, but may never be emptied into drains.

2. Mattresses, straw palliasses, pillows, upholstered furniture and similar items must be shaken or beaten for at least one hour in the open air (if rainy at least 2 hours in the hall) under the supervision of the fumigation chief.

3. If possible the stuffing of straw palliasses should be changed. The old stuffing may not however be burnt, but may be re-used after it has been aired for a further period.

4. Should the chimneys have been covered from above, these coverings must be removed carefully since otherwise there is a danger that the fires in the stoves and hearths will not have sufficient draught, which may cause carbon monoxide poisoning.

5. After the final release has been made, two copies of a fumigation report are to be filled in in the prescribed manner. The following points in particular should be shown:

a) Volume of fumigated rooms.

b) Amount of Zyklon used.

c) Name of fumigation chief.

d) Names of other personnel.

e) Time required for gas to take effect.

f) Time at which dis-infested rooms were released.

XIV. Final Release.

1. Under no circumstances less than 21 hours after airing was started.

2. All items removed for beating are to be taken back into the room.

3. Doors and windows to be closed for one hour.

4. In rooms with heating facilities a temperature of at least 15 deg. Cent. must be produced.

145

5. Gas detecting. The paper strip may not show a darker blue than the lightest colour, even between blankets and mattresses which have been placed on top of each other, or in rooms which are not easily accessible and which it is difficult to air. Should this not be the case, airing must be continued and the check for gas repeated after a few hours.

6. The check for gas must be made in each room of buildings which are again to be used as sleeping accommodation as soon as possible. Under no circumstances may anyone sleep in a room which has been fumigated in the night following the fumigation. The windows must always remain open during the first night that the room is used again.

7. The fumigation chief or his deputy may not leave the building until the very last room has been finally released.

146

Issued by the Health Institution

of the Protectorate Bohemia and

Moravia in Prague.

CERTIFICATE OF TRANSLATION.

I, DOROTHEA L. GALEWSKI, ETO # 34079, hereby certify that I am thoroughly conversant with the English and German languages; and that the above is a true and correct translation of Document No. NI-9912.

DOROTHEA L. GALEWSKI
ETO 34079

STAFF EVIDENCE ANALYSIS   By: A.H.Elbau
                                           Date: 21 August 1947

Document No.   NI-9913

Title and/or general nature: Dispatch notes from the Dessauer
                                          Werke fuer Zucker-und Chemische
                                          Industrie A.G., Dessau, to Deutsche
                                          Gesellschaft fuer Schaedlings-
                                          bekaempfung m.b.H., Frankfurt/Main,
                                          re delivery of Zyklon B to (1)
                                          concentration camps Oranienburg and
                                          Auschwitz (2) sundry customers.

Date: (1) 11 April 1944, 12 May 1944, 26
                                          May 1944, 11 April 1944, 27 April
                                          1944.
                                          (2) 26 September 1944 to 11 January
                                          1945

Doc. 6

Source (Location of original, etc.):   Source: DEGESCH, Schaumainkai 43,   147
                                          Frankfurt/Main
                                          Location: Document Control Branch,
                                          OCCWC, Nuernberg, Germany

PERSONS, FIRMS OR ORGANIZATIONS INVOLVED:

                          NI- IG Farben
                          NI- IGF Dessauer Werke f. Zucker-u.
                                  Chemische Industrie A.G.
                          NI- IGF DEGESCH
                          NC- Concentration camp Oranienburg
                          NC- Concentration camp Auschwitz

TO BE FILED UNDER THESE REFERENCE HEADINGS:
                          As above. Also:

                          NI- IGF Poison Gas
                          NI- IGF Atrocities

SUMMARY (Indicate page numbers):   (63 pages)

                          See title.

                                End

(page 1 of original)

Dessauer Werke fuer Zucker-
und Chemische Industrie
Aktiengesellschaft   Dessau,   11 April 1944

                    To:

                         Deutsche Gesellschaft fuer Schaedlingsbekaempfung
                              m.b.H.

Subject: Zyklon Degesch-order   Frankfurt a. Main
Your order No: 193 (March/44)
Dessau No: April delivery

                    Boe.
                         Invoice for

                         Zyklon B Poison

148   Declared as Prussic acid (Hydrocyanic acid), water content at most 3%,
       completely absorbed in a porous medium. Poison.

             To-day, we dispatched by rail, carriage forward, to:
             Concentration camp Oranienburg, Disinfection and
             Disinfestation Department,

             Railroad station: _Oranienburg_
                      _as freight

             under Wehrmacht bill of lading from H.St. Verw. Dessau -
                                        Rosslau.

                              - 1 -

(page 1 of original cont'd)

Crates No. Type	No	Containing per size can	Total No of cans	Kg % CN total	Cross weight per crate	Total weight gross tare net	Remarks
13 67.49 .34,5	501,59/ 71	(1,425) 30 500 152/120	390	195	64	832 276,25 555,75	Erco with- out indicator

D.G.S.
Poison
Death's
Head

Freight charge

RM 6,95

The labels bear the stamp:

"Take care, no indicator ! "

149

13				195		832 276,25 555,75	

Dessauer Werke

fuer Zucker- und Chemische

Industrie

Aktiengesellschaft

Signatures and initials
illegible

- 2 -

(page 2 of original)

Dessauer Werke fuer Zucker-
und Chemische Industrie
Aktiengesellschaft   Dessau,   12 May 1944

                    To

                         Deutsche Gesellschaft fuer Schaedlingsbekaempfung
                         m.b.H.

                              Frankfurt a.Main_

Subject: Zyklon Degesch-order
Your order No: 193/ March/ 44
Dessau No: May delivery_

                         Invoice for

                    Zyklon B Poison

150

Declared as Prussic acid (Hydrocyanic acid), water content at most 3%,
completely absorbed in a porous medium. Poison.

          To-day, we dispatched by rail, carriage forward, to:
          Concentration camp Oranienburg, Disinfection and
          Disinfestation Department,

               Railroad_ station:_Oranienburg

                    _as freight

under Wehrmacht bill of lading from senior rank of the Wehrmacht at
Dessau.

(page 1 of original cont'd)

Crates No. Type	No Containing per size can	Total No of cans	Kg % CN total	Gross weight per crate	Total weight gross tare net	Remarks
13 67.49 .34,5	50 133/(1,425) 45 30 500 152/120	390	195	64	832 276,25 555,75	Erco without indicato

D.G.S.
Poison
Death's
Head

Freight charge
RM 6,95

The labels bear the stamp:
"Take care , no indicator !"

151

13			195		832 276,25 555,75	

Dessauer Werke
fuer Zucker- und Chemische
Industrie
Aktiengesellschaft

Illegible initials

(page 3 of original)

Dessauer Werke fuer Zucker-
und Chemische Industrie
Aktiengesellschaft.   Dessau,   26 May 1944

            To

                Deutsche Gesellschaft fuer Schädlingsbekaempfung m. b.H.

                    Frankfurt a. Main

Subject: Zyklon Degesch-order
Your order No: 193/March/44
Dessau No: June (delivery)

                    Bce./Fu.

152   Invoice for

                    Zyklon   B   Poison

Declared as Prussic acid (Hydrocyanic acid), water content at most 3%,
completely absorbed in a porous medium, Poison.

        To-day, we dispatched by rail, carriage forward, to:
        Concentration camp Oranienburg, Disinfection and
        Disinfestation Department,

        Railroad station: Oranienburg

                as freight

                        from
under Wehrmacht bill of lading/senior rank of the Wehrmacht at Dessau
in your name.

(page 3 of original cont'd)

Crates No. Type	No. Containing per size can	Total No. of cans	Kg % CN total	Gross weight per crate	Total weight gross tare net	Remarks
13 67.49 .34,5	50198/(1,425) 210 30 500 152/120	390	195	64	832 276,25 555,75	

Free

without
indicator

D.G.S.
Poison
Death's
Head

153

Freight charges
RM 4,95

The labels bear the stamp:

"Take care, no indicator! "

13			195		832 276,25 555,75	

Dessauer Werke

fuer Zucker- und Chemische

Industrie

Aktiengesellschaft

Signature and initials
illegible

(page 4 of original)

Dessauer Werke fuer Zucker-
und Chemische Industrie
Aktiengesellschaft   Dessau, 11 April 1944

                    To

                    Deutsche Gesellschaft faer Schaedlingsbekaempfung
                              m.b.H.

                         Frankfurt a. Main

Subject: Zyklon Degesch-order
Your order No: 192 (April delivery)
Dessau No: (March/44)

                         Bce.

154
                    Invoice for

                    Zyklon B Poison

Declared as Prussic acid (Hydrocyanic acid), water content at most 3%,
completely absorbed in a porous medium. Poison.

        To-day, we dispatched by rail, carriage forward, to:
        Concentration camp Auschwitz, Disinfection and
        Disinfestation Department,

        Railroad station: _Auschwitz_

              as_freight

under Wehrmacht bill of lading from H.St. Verw. Dessau - Rosslau.

(page 4 of original cont'd)

- -

Crates	No.	Containing per size can (1,425)		Total No of cans	Kg % GN total	Gross weight per crate	Total weight gross tare net			Remarks
No. Type										
13 67.49 .34,5	50146/ 58	30 152/120	500	390	195	64	832	276,25	555,75	Erco

without
indicator

D.G.S.
Poison
Death's
Head

Freight charge

_RM 6,95_

155

The labels bear the stamp:

"Take care, no indicator!_"

- -

13					195		832	276,25	555,75

- -

Dessauer Werke

fuer Zucker- und Chemische Industrie

Aktiengesellschaft

Signature and initials
illegible.

(page 5 of original)

Dessauer Werke fuer Zucker-
und Chemische Industrie
Aktiengesellschaft   Dessau,   27 April 1947

                    To

                         Deutsche Gesellschaft fuer Schaedlingsbekaempfung
                                   m.b.H.

                              Frankfurt a.Main

Subject: Zyklon Degesch-order
Your order No: 192/March 44
Dessau No: (May-delivery)

                         Boe.

156
                         Invoice for

                         Zyklon B Poison

Declared as Prussic acid (Hydrocyanic acid), water content at most 3%,
completely absorbed in a porous medium, Poison.

To-day, we dispatched by rail, carriage forward, to:
Concentration camp Auschwitz, Disinfection and
Disinfestation Department,

                    Railroad station: Auschwitz

                         as freight

(page 5 of original cont'd)

Crates No.	Containing per size can	Total No of cans	Kg % CN total	Gross weight per crate	Total weight gross tare net	Remarks
No.Type	(1,425)					
13 67.49	50 72/30 500	390	195	64 832	276,25 555,75	Erco
.34,5	84 152/120					without indicator

D.G.S.
Poison
Death's
Head

Freight charge

RM 6,95   157

The labels bear the stamp:

"Take care, no indicator!"

13			195	832	276,25 555,75	

Dessauer Werke

Signature and initials   fuer Zucker- und Chemische Industrie
    illegible.
                                Aktiengesellschaft

- 10 -

CERTIFICATE OF TRANSLATION

5 November 1947

I, Arthur MCNAMARA, Civ.No. 20191, hereby certify, that I am a duly appointed translator for the German and English languages and that the above is a true and correct translation of excerpts from the document No. NI-9913-A.

Arthur MCNAMARA
Civ.No. 20191

158

STAFF EVIDENCE ANALYSIS

BY: Haeni
DATE: 17 Oct 1947

DOCUMENT No.

NI 11 906

TITLE AND/OR GENERAL NATURE:

Copy of letter Kaliwerke Kolin
to Sicherheitspolizei Theresienstadt, concerning the deliveries of Cyclon B.

DATE:

28 Febr 1944

SOURCE (Location of original, etc.):

Folder No. 501
Kaliwerke Kolin A.G., Kolin
near Prague.

Doc. 7

159

PERSONS, FIRMS OR ORGANIZATIONS INVOLVED:

see below

TO BE FILED UNDER THESE REFERENCE HEADINGS:

NI – IGF DEGESCH
NI – IGF poison gas.
NI – IGF KALIWERKE KOLIN

SUMMARY (Indicate page numbers):

Letter states that Theresienstadt needs 75 kg of Cyclon B a week. Until
further notice, Kaliwerke Kolin will send monthly shipments of 300 kg of
Cyclon B to Theresienstadt.
(Copy of the letter was sent to DEGESCH, Prague.)

E N D

To the Commander of the Security Police and
the SD (Security Service)

Theresienstadt.

Z. II/2 Ve. 44/Scha   25 Feb 44   KJ/S   28 Feb 1944

Zyklon B-Supplies.

      We herewith acknowledge receipt of your above letter and
have noted that 75 kg Zyklon B per week will cover your require-
ments.

      As of 1 March of this year we will supply this amount to
you every week until further notice, and hope you will be agreeable
to our sending off a month's supply, 300 kg., at that time, to
facilitate dispatch.

                        KALIWERKE AKTIENGESELLSCHAFT
                           (two illegible initials)

160

Copy to Degesch, Pag.

CERTIFICATE OF TRANSLATION

I, DOROTHEA L. GALEWSKI, ETO #34079, hereby certify that I am
thoroughly conversant with the English and German languages; and
that the above is a true and correct translation of Document No.
NI-11906.

                        Dorothea L. GALEWSKI,
                        ETO #34079.

-1-

Interrogation-Nr. 929 B

V E R N E H M U N G

von Herrn Kurt B E C H E R ,
am 10. Juli 1947, von 11 - 12 Uhr,
durch Mr. Curt PONGER,
in Anwesenheit von Herrn Dr. KASTNER,
auf Veranlassung von Mr. HART, SS-Sektion.
Stenographin: M. Fritsche.

1.Fr. Herr BECHER ich moechte unser letztes Gespraech fortsetzen. Sie werden sich

noch erinnern, wo wir abbrechen mussten; die Rede war, dieses Raetsel "Buda-

pester Ghetto".

A. Herr Dr. KASTNER, Sie werden verstehen, dass ich unter dem Eindruck Sie nach

dieser langen Zeit wieder zu sehen, ziemlich beeindruckt war und bin. Sie   *Doc. 8*

werden deswegen verstehen, dass ich einfach physisch nicht in der Lage bin   161

Ihnen jeweils so klar die Dinge zu beantworten, in einer Vernehmung, wie ich

es tun wuerde, wenn wir unter anderen Umstaenden ueber die Dinge sprechen

wuerden. Ich habe nun 2 Tage Zeit gehabt ueber die Dinge nachzudenken und

ich glaube, ich kann Ihnen Einiges sagen, was Sie wissen wollen, wenn ich

Ihnen auch sagen darf, dass ich an sich eben diese Art der Vernehmung -

2.Fr. Darueber wollen wir uns nicht aufhalten.

A. Ich bitte aber zu beruecksichtigen, dass, bevor Budapest eingeschlossen wur-

de, mein Aufgabengebiet vom Gesichtspunkt der Ungarn, der Schwerpunkt auf

dem Manfred-WEISS-Konzern lag und dass schliesslich viele einzelne Interven-

tionen nur ein Teilgebiet meiner Sorge um die Fortsetzung meiner grossen

Linie in der Judenangelegenheit war. Sie werden deswegen verstehen, dass ich

mich nicht an jedes Detail erinnern kann. Fuer mich gab es nur eine grosse

Linie und da muessen Sie mir gestatten darueber nachzudenken. Ich bitte mir

die Fragen zu stellen.

3.Fr. Ich gehe nicht auf das ein, was Sie sagten, nur um Zeit zu ersparen.

A. Die Frage des "Budapester Ghetto's" sehe ich wie folgt: Sie erinnern sich
unserer Eroerterung anfangs November in Zuerich und St.Gallen und im Schnell-
zug und ich moechte anregen, dass Herr EICHMANN den letzten Versuch machte,
den Befehl HIMMLER'S, der zweifelsohne durch Sie und mich erwirkt worden ist,
zu durchbrechen; versuchte wurde Herrn VEESEMAYER bei der ungarischen Regie-
rung in engster Zusammenarbeit mit den Pfeilkreuzlern die Deportation der
Juden fortzusetzen durch Wien. Dass das kein Arbeitseinsatz der Schutzstel-
lung war, ging daraus hervor, dass er Frauen und Kinder und Kinder von 15,
ja 13 Jahren aufwaerts und Greise nahm. Wir waren uns darueber einig, dass
ich zunaechst unmittelbar erwirkte, dass diese Altersgrenzen geaendert wurden
Herr DR.KASTNER, ich bitte weiter sich daran zu erinnern, Herr Dr.BILLITZ
fuhr bereits von Zuerich zurueck. Ich glaube wir sind zusammengefahren und
erinnere mich, dass wir in einer langen Nacht sehr eingehend ueber die Dinge
gesprochen haben. Ich fuhr 3 Tage spaeter zu HIMMLER; ich nahm Herrn WINKEL-
MANN mit. Ich sagte zu WINKELMANN, - zu meinem Fahrer WOLF alle halbe Stunde
eine Panne, - als die Elendsmaersche vorbeizogen, glauben sie, dass diese
Kinder, diese Mutter und dieser Greis noch nach Wien kommt? Ich habe bei
HIMMLER die Abstoppung des Fussmarsches erwirkt.

4.Fr. Wann?

A. Sagen Sie mir, wann wir wir nach Budapest zurueckgekommen sind.

5.Fr. Am 8.November.

A. Ich habe eine laengere Einreisegenehmigung in die Schweiz. Ich habe am sel-
ben Tag ein Fernschreiben an HIMMLER abgefasst, wo ich meinen Eindruck schil-
derte, was ich auf der Strasse gesehen habe. Ich bin 3 Tage spaeter zu HIMMLER
gefahren, ich glaube er war in Ostpreussen; es wurde dort im Beisein von

A. WINKELMANN das Verbot des weiteren Abtransportes des Fussmarsches befohlen.
Dieser Befehl ging an EICHMANN und zwar von WINKELMANN an EICHMANN. Ich bitte Sie sich zu erinnern, dass urspruenglich die Ghettorisierung gemacht worden ist, um die Juden zum Abmarsch bereit zu haben. Ich erinnere mich, dass
Herr EICHMANN bei mir war und mir gesagt hat, es waere ihm von VEESEMAYER
nur ein Kontingent von 25 Tausend gegeben worden. Das ist eine Bestaetigung,
dass VEESEMAYER eingeschaltet war.

Fr. Fuer mich ist VEESEMAYER'S Rolle niemals ein Fragezeichen gewesen.

A. Da ich ja um ihn herumgehen musste, weil er mein Gegner war, deswegen musste
ich ja ohne VEESEMAYER gehen. Das sind Punkte, die authentisch sind. Der
Sinn von Herrn EICHMANN war, gegen den Befehl zu handeln, den ich ihm ja
selbst von HIMMLER gezeigt habe. Dann habe ich ihn Herrn BILLITZ gezeigt.
Ich weiss nicht, ob Sie das wissen?

Fr. Ich weiss, dass Sie das BILLITZ gezeigt haben. Er hat mit mir gesprochen.

A. Herr EICHMANN wollte damals die letzten 150 Tausend Juden aus Ungarn heraus -
bringen. Ich weiss auch, dass er mir gesagt hat, ich habe die Zusage von 50
Tausend, die Durchfuehrung ist meine Sache. Er hat mich verhoehnt; Sie kennen
seine sarkastische Art. So ist das Ghetto in Budapest entstanden, wenn man
es Ghetto nennen wollte. Ich kannte es mehr unter dem Namen einer Zusammen-
gruppierung. Als ich bei HIMMLER war, hat mich LUEBEN einmal angerufen und
mich darauf aufmerksam gemacht, dass Herr EICHMANN zusammen mit den Pfeilkreuzlern andere Dinge im Spiele haette. Ich kann mich auf den Wortlaut nicht
besinnen, aber ich darf Ihnen sagen, auf der Leitung Budapest-Fuehrerhaupt-
quartier konnte Herr LUEBEN auch keinen Klartext sprechen. LUEBEN hielt es
fuer notwendig mich im Fuehrerhauptquartier anzurufen. Sie hatten einen bes-

163

A. seren Nachrichtendienst in Budapest. Ich weiss nicht, ob Sie wissen, dass der ungarische Honved-General im Manfred-Weiss-Werk abgefuehrt werden soll te und ich den General durch das Werk gefuehrt habe und ganz Budapest darueber gestaunt hat. Ich habe auch WINKELMANN gegenueber meine Einstellung zur pfeilkreuzlerischen Partei nicht verschwiegen. Ich habe damals in verfolgter Linie, die ich ja spaeter bewiesen habe, sowohl Intervention bei Herrn WINKELMANN und mit Herrn WINKELMANN bei Herrn KOVARCZ gefuehrt und gesagt, was fuer Vollmachten ich von HIMMLER habe. Alle die anderen Herren, die seinerzeit bei mir gewesen sind, koennen das bezeugen. Es ist damals unter dem Einfluss Ihrer Herren, die nicht ein Mal sondern praktisch ununterbrochen mein Vorzimmer belagert haben, erreicht worden, dass zunaechst nichts in Beudapest erfolgt ist und dass diePfle Pfeilkreuzler in Schach gehalten worden sind. Dass z.B. am 16. oder 17. 3 Tausend Juden aus ihren Wohnungen herausgeholt und ermordert worden sind, das habe ich auch nicht gewusst. Ich weiss jedenfalls, dass unter dem staendigen Eindruck, den die Herren Dr.BILLITZ und Sie und Ihre Mitarbeiter vermittelt haben, zunaechst alles abgewendet wurde, was in der Zeit bis zum 24.Dezember moeglich war. Sie haben mich gefragt, ob ich mich an die Funksprueche erinnere, die Herr KETTLITZ ueber Bregenz geschickt hat nach unserer Abreise. Ich erinnere mich nicht an den Wortlaut; ich erinnere mich daran, dass diese Funksprueche mich veranlasst haben, Sie zu bitten, nach Bregenz zu fahren. Sie muessen wisseh, dass mein Spiel HIMMLER gegenueber nicht ganz einfach war.

8.Fr. Augenblick. Das stimmt naemlich nicht. Sie haben wahrscheinlich diesen Telegrammwechsel aus Ihrem Gedaechtnis verloren.

164

A. Ich darf jetzt auf folgendes ueberspringen. Ich weiss nicht, ob ich es
Ihnen damals gesagt habe, dass ich HIMMLER im November 1944 gesagt habe,-

.Fr. Nadh unserer Rueckkehr aus der Schweiz?

A. Gelegentlich meiner Anwesenheit bei ihm, nachdem ich den Fussmarsch abgestoppt hatte.

O.Fr. Das Datum duerfte zwischen dem 20. und 26.November gewesen sein. Ich

A. Ich darf Ihnen sagen, trotzdem ich versucht habe auf diplomatischem Weg
mit Herrn EICHMANN zu verkehren, habe ich HIMMLER gesagt, dass ich immer
wieder feststellen muss, dass EICHMANN den von ihm gegebenen Befehl sabotiert. Den Fussmarsch, den er arrangiert hat, war ein reines Morden.

1.Fr. Sie hatten im November 1944 einen Besuch in Budapest und zwar einen hoehe-
ren Gast. Erinnern Sie sich noch?   165

A. Ja.

2.Fr. Wer war das ?

A. Herr JUETTNER.

3.Fr. Wissen Sie, wer noch?

A. Ausserdem war seinerzeit da Herr GEHARDT. In seiner Umgebung war sein Adjutant, ein Obersturmbannfuehrer.

4.Fr. Ich habe GEBHARDT mal gesehen. Er hat einige lustige Tage in Budapest ver-
lebt. Vielleicht nicht in seiner Umgebung, aber irgendjemand in seiner Begleitung?

A. Ein Ungar?

5.Fr. Nein. Der Kommandant von Auschwitz, Obersturmbannfuehrer HOESS.

A. Da muss ich Ihnen sagen, ich kenne HOESS nicht und habe ihn auch nicht gesehen. Ich weiss aber, dass er einpaar mal da war.

16.Fr. HOESS war bei Dr.BILLITZ und hat sich sehr abfaellig ueber den Fussmarsch geaeussert.

A. Das habe ich nicht gewusst. HOESS war bei uns im Buero, das weiss ich nicht

17.Fr. Das hat mir Dr.BILLITZ gesagt. Die Frage, die ich in diesem Zusammenhang stellen will, ist, Herr JÜTTNER hat auch den Fussmarsch gesehen. Hat er nichts darueber zu sagen gehabt?

A. JUETTNER war vor meiner Reise zu HIMMER da. Deswegen bin ich nicht gleich gereist, weil er da war und JUETTNER hat den Fussmarsch auch missbilligt.

18.Fr. Erinnern Sie sich, ob aus dieser Missbilligung damals irgendwelche Konsequenzen an Ort und Stelle betrieben worden sind?

A. Ich glaube, dass JUETTNER HIMMLER ebenfalls -

19.Fr. Herr BECHER, die Sache ist nur am Rande erwaehnt. Ich werde Ihnen sagen, was damals gespielt worden ist. EICHMANN war in diesem Augenblick nicht in Budapest. Herr JUETTNER hat jemand beauftragt, den Stellvertreter EICHMANN' dazu zu bringen, dass der Fussmarsch abgestoppt wird. Nach Rueckkehr EICHmann's nach Budapest, hat EICHMANN den Befehl ignoriert. Vielleicht koennen Sie sich nicht an Einzelheiten erinnern.

A. Herr Dr.KASTNER, ich weiss, dass der Nachrichtendienst auch in Bezug auf "BECHER" gut war und ich hatte ueber Budapest in Dr.BILLITZ den besten Nachrichtenapparat.

20.Fr. An HOESS erinnern Sie sich nicht?

A. Nein.

21.Fr. Das war naemlich pikant. - Wer war Dr.BILLITZ?

A. Ein Jude, der immer an meiner Seite sass und in Budapest von einem Ministerium zum anderen fuhr.

22.Fr. Sie kannten JUETTNER und HOESS vom Hauptquartier HITLER'S?

166

A.   Nein. Ich habe ihn in Wien abgeholt, schon mit dem Gedanken, dass er den
      Fussmarsch sieht. Ich habe JUETTNER mal im Hotel Imperial in Wien erwar-
      tet und ich habe ihn in einem Auto nach Budapest gebracht und habe ihm
      den Fussmarsch gezeigt.

23.Fr. Was hat er dazu gesagt?

A.   JUETTNER war empoert, wenn er auch SS-Obergruppenfuehrer war.

24.Fr. Glauben Sie, dass fuer JUETTNER so ein Anblick neu war?

A.   Ja.

25.Fr. Es ist ein Unterschied, was sich hinter dem Stacheldraht abspielt und was
      in der Welt auf der Landstrasse passiert.

A.   Herr PONGER, ich darf Ihnen eines sagen, dass gegen mich alles gestanden
      ist. Ich habe deswegen auch nicht meinen besten Freunden sagen koennen,
      was ist und was ich mache.

                                                                                    167

26.Fr. Kommen wir zurueck zu dem Thema. Das ist das, was Sie ueber Budapest wis-
      sen?

A.   Ich sah also, dass EICHMANN ununterbrochen selbst oder durch seine Leute
      versuchte kleine Brocken herauszubeissen. Ich habe damals HIMMLER gesagt,
      obwohl ich monatelang veructh habe, mich mit EICHMANN nicht zu ueberwerfen,
      ich komme gegen die Sabotagen EICHMANN'S nicht mehr an. HIMMLER hat zu
      mir gesagt, bleiben Sie hier und lassen Sie den EICHMANN kommen. Ich sagte,
      ich kann nicht hier bleiben. Ich muss zurueck nach Budapest. Dann sagte
      HIMMLER, dann bringen Sie ihn das naechstemal mit.

27.Fr. Ich moechte Sie auf etwas aufmerksam machen. Am 30. November 1944 habe
      ich Budapest verlassen in Begleitung von KRELL in Richtung Schweizer Gren-
      ze, Besprechung SALLY MAYER, wegen dem 2.Telegramm von KALLITZ, da er an
      Sie gerichtet hat mit dem Text, SALLY MAYER unerreichbar, Sache laeuft

27.Fr. nicht. Vorangehend eine Besprechung in Maria Valeria im Beisein von EICH-

MANN und Dr.BILLITZ, wo diese Reise entschieden wurde.

A. Jawohl.

28.Fr. Vielleicht werden Sie sich an ein Detail erinnern. Ich bin heraus gegangen

dann wurde ich zurueckgerufen und fand EICHMANN allein vor und er begann

mit mir ueber meine Familie zu sprechen, ob meine Familie ebenfalls mit

der Gruppe Bergen-Belsen verlassen darf. Erinnern Sie sich?

A. Die ganze Unterhaltung ist mir nicht klar. EICHMANN sprach mit Ihnen al-

lein ueber die Erpressung Ihrer Familie, Ihrer Freunde.

29.Fr. Ich nehme an, erstmals wollte er Ihre Zustimmung dazu haben. Sie haben

wahrscheinlich abgelehnt; da versuchte er meine Zustimmung einzuholen.

168 Das habe ich mir so logisch ausgerechnet. Sie haben ein festes Verspre-

chen gemacht, meine Familie mitfahren zu lassen?

A. Ja. Ich weiss es genau. Sie waren in sehr grosser Sorge und haben BILLITZ

gesagt, BECHER hat mir gesagt bezw. Garantien gegeben, dass meine Familie

mitfahren darf.

30.Fr. Erinnern Sie sich, wass BILLITZ verlangt hat oder an etwas Aehnlichem?

A. Koennen Sie mir eine Andeutung machen.

31.Fr. Ich weiss nicht, was geschehen ist, als ich Ihr Buero verlassen hatte.

Ich weiss nur, dass ich nach ungefaehr 5 Minuten zurueckgerufen wurde

und da fand ich EICHMANN allein vor und EICHMANN sagte mir, "Sie fahren

jetzt zur Schweizer Grenze, ich lasse Ihre Familie in Bergen-Belsen zu-

rueckhalten.

A. Eines war klar. Herr EICHMANN wollte nicht, dass ich Sie fahren liess.

EICHMANN hat mir von Anfang an gesagt, den Kopf von dem KASTNER will ich

haben.

32.Fr. Warum?

A. Er hat Sie gehasst. Sie waren doch der einzigste Exponent, der gegen ihn stand.

33.Fr. Er hat vielleicht den Wert meines Kopfes ueberschaetzt.

A. Nein. Der ganze Ablauf dieser Unterhaltung ist mir klar.

34.Fr. Wann wollte er meinen Kopf haben?

A. Noch am 15.April. Bevor wir nach Bergen-Belsen fuhren, mussten wir in der Kurfuerstenstrasse anhalten, weil ich die Formalitaeten erfuellen musste. Da hat EICHMANN zu mir gesagt, "ich lasse Sie nicht nach Bergen-Belsen hinein." Ich sagte, doch und zwar in Begleitung von Dr.KASTNER. Er sagte, "auch nicht mit Befehl HIMMLER'S". Ich sagte, gut, dann spreche ich mit Herrn MUELLER. Sie sassen im Auto. Ich wurde aber von Herrn MUELLER nicht empfangen. Dann sagte ich zu EICHMANN, "ich fahre mit Dr.KASTNER nach Bergen-Belsen." Damals hat EICHMANN noch mir und Ihnen gegenueber die Karten nicht aufdecken wollen. Nun moechte ich Ihnen noch Einiges sagen ueber die gemeinsame Besprechung bei HIMMLER mit EICHMANN, im Quartier in Triberg.

169

35.Fr. Wann?

A. Es muss gewesen sein in der 1.Haelfte im Dezember.

36.Fr. Das duerfte nicht in der 1.Dez.-Woche gewesen sein.

A. Ich sage in der 1.Haelfte. Ich bin am 18.Dezember wieder von Budapest wegefahren, also um den 13.Dezember duerfte es gewesen sein.

37.Fr. Ich glaube, dass ich das letzte Telegramm von Ihnen aus Budapest in Bregenz gegen den 10. oder 11. erhalten habe. Dann duerfte es zwischen dem 12. und 18.Dezember gewesen sein.

A. Ich moechte Ihnen einen sehr starken Ausbruch schildern. Herr HIMMLER hat in meinem Beisein Herrn EICHMANN 10 Minuten empfangen und ihn ange-

A. schrieen, "wenn Sie bisher Juden ermordet haben und ich Ihnen jetzt befehle Juden zu pflegen, dann erklaeren Sie mir, ob Sie diesen Befehl von mir ausfuehren oder nicht". Ich bin damals beinahe in die Knie gegangen, was das bei Herrn EICHMANN gegen mich und ende unsere Sache ausloest. Herr EICHMANN hat gesagt, "jawohl Reichsfuehrer" und ist versteinert. HIMMLER hat ihn dann nach weiteren Besprechungen, ca. von 10 Minuten Dauer, entlassen und ich bin bei ihm geblieben. Ich habe dann HIMMLER beinahe auf den Knieen gebeten, "um Gottes Willen biegen Sie das mit EICHMANN, bevor er hier Ihr Quartier verlaesst, wieder gerade; der Mann macht alles gegen Ihre Befehle und macht weitere Sachen". Es ist fuer Sie wahrscheinlich kein Geheimnis geblieben, dass ich mit allen Mitteln gespielt habe, die es gibt. Ich habe damals aus meiner Not und Angst heraus zu HIMMLER gesagt, "ich weiss einen Weg, um nicht das Gegenteil bei EICHMANN auszuloesen und was Sie mit Ihrem Befehl ausgeloest haben, verleihen Sie ihm das Kriegsverdienstkreuz I.Kl. mit Schwertern! HIMMLER sagte, "das kommt nicht in Frage, der Kerl fuehrt meine Befehle nicht aus! Und dann habe ich gesagt, "Reichsfuehrer, ich bitte Sie noch einmal der Sache wegen". Er sagte, "meinetwegen verleihen Sie dem EICHMANN das Kriegsverdienstkreuz I.Kl. mit Schwertern. Dann ist Herrn EICHMANN das Kriegsverdienstkreuz I.Kl. mit Schwertern verliehen worden und Herr EICHMANN war versoehnt. Das ist eine "story", die ich noch niemals erzaehlt habe.

38. Fr. War er versoehnt?
                    damit
A. Sie wissen, was ich meine. Alle die kleinen Sachen, die er haette noch machen koennen, die haette er aber in vermehrtem Masse gemacht, wenn dieser fuerchterliche "Anschiess" von HIMMLER sitzen geblieben waere.

39. Fr: Eine Paradoxie ist, wenn in der damaligen deutschen Konzentration der klein

9.Fr. Obersturmbannfuehrer EICHMANN den allmaechtigen Reichsfuehrer-SS -

A. beschiess, entschuldigen Sie bitte, dass ist es nicht und ist es doch.
Ich glaube einigermassen Einblick gehabt zu haben. Zum Schluss sagte
mir mal EICHMANN, "ich fuehre die Befehle des Gruppenfuehrers MUELLER
aus und ich fuehre die Befehle HIMMLER'S aus, aber bevor ich die Befehle
HIMMLER'S ausfuehre, bespreche ich sie noch mit MUELLER. Selbstverstaendlich hat EICHMANN die Befehle HIMMLER'S ausgefuehrt, aber er ist dabei
immer den Weg gegangen, der ihm am meisten zusagte; und bei der Fuelle
und Oberflaechlichkeit, die ich bei HIMMLER festgestellt habe, glaube
ich, dass fuer EICHMANN immer soviel Spielraum da war, dass er doch
schliesslich seinen Willen sehr stark durchgesetzt hat.

0.Fr. Herr Dr.KASTNER, ich moechte Sie kurz unterbrechen und Herrn BECHER um
einige Sachen fragen bezuegl. EICHMANN. - Wann hatten Sie EICHMANN das
1.x gesehen?

A. Im Maerz/April 1944.

1.Fr. Wussten Sie damals wer EICHMANN war?

A. Nein.

2.Fr. Was hoerten Sie ueber EICHMANN'S Taetigkeit das 1.x?

A. Ich hoerte zunaechst ueber EICHMANN'S Taetigkeit, dass er in der Judenangelegenheit taetig war.

3.Fr. Sie wussten, dass er Referent von Judenangelegenheiten war?

A. Ja, nach einigen Tagen habe ich das festgestellt.

4.Fr. Hatten Sie sich mal mit EICHMANN ueber diese Vorgeschichte der ganzen
Judenvernichtung oder Fragen unterhalten?

A. Nein. Ich erklaere Ihnen, dass EICHMANN mir zum 1.x zugegeben hat, dass
Juden vernichtet werden bezw. worden sind, in dem Moment, als ich ihm

171

A. den Befehl von HIMMLER vorgelegt habe, dass die Vernichtung abzustoppen sei.

45.Fr. Sie wussten von der Judenvernichtung vor diesem Gespraech mit EICHMANN, wo er Ihnen das zugegeben hat?

A. Ich wusste das unbestaetigt von Dr.KASTNER und SALLY MAYER. Ich haette ja nicht einen Gegenbefehl erwirken koennen, wenn ich nicht gewusst haette, dass einer da war. Als ich HIMMLER sagte, dass mir kuerzlich in der Schweiz an Hand von vielen Beispielen gesagt wurde, dass Judenvernichtungen vorkommen, sagte HIMMLER zu mir, das sei Verlaeumdung und Internationale Propaganda.

46.Fr. Nachdem Sie wussten, dass Judenvernichtungen vorkamen, haben Sie sich jemals den Kopf zerbrochen, wer der Repraesentant dieser Judenvernichtungen war?

A. EICHMANN war der fanatische Handlanger, der geistige Traeger war er aber nicht.

47.Fr. Glauben Sie, dass das auf HIMMLER'S Mist gewachsen ist?

A. HIMMLER hat nicht soviel Geist, aber ich glaube, dass ~~HIMMLER einer~~ HITLER der Maenner war. Ich glaube Herr Dr.KASTNER, wir haben auch mal darueber gesprochen.

48.Fr. Viel haben wir darueber nicht sprechen koennen. -
Sie haben immer versucht HIMMLER'S Rolle in dieser Angelegenheit als eine sympathische hinzustellen.

A. Musste ich das nicht?

49.Fr. Das ist ganz richtig. Herr BECHER, schauen Sie, Sie wissen heute ungefaehr alles, was gelaufen ist.

A. Ja, ich war ungefaehr 10 Monate lang hier Dolmetscher, man koennte aus-

A. spucken.

.Fr. Ich spreche von den nuechternen Tatsachen. Es ist heute kein Geheimnis

mehr, dass ueber 6 Millionen Juden vernichtet worden sind. Sie haben einen

Einblick in diese Maschine gehabt, die da oeben stand?

A. Ja.

.Fr. Sie glauben also HIMMLER?

A. Ja, HIMMLER, BORMANN. BORMANN war ja der absolute boese Geist. Das sage

ich nicht, weil BORMANN tot ist oder nicht da ist. Ich glaube schon, dass
en
BORMANN ein sehr, sehr starken Einfluss hatte und Gegenspieler und Intri-

gant der anderen war.
                     HITLER
.Fr. Sie glauben, EICHMANN, HITLER, BORMANN?

A. EICHMANN war nur der Handlanger. Ich lasse auch HIMMLER nicht aus.   173

.Fr. Die SS war doch zumindest der Traeger?

A. Ich moechte Ihnen dazu folgendes sagen: Selbstverstaendlich waren es

HITLER, BORMANN, HIMMLER usw..

.Fr. Auf welche Unterstuetzung konnte EICHMANN rechnen?

A. Das war HIMMLER. Ich weiss nicht, ob es stimmt, aber man erzaehlt hier,

dass EICHMANN und dieser HOESS einen persoenlichen Draht zur sogenannten

Kanzlei des Fuehrers hatten. Das ist eine reine "story"; und dass der

HOESS mal mit BORMANN befreundet war.

.Fr. Das stammt vielleicht von den Kreisen des W.V.H.A.?

A. Wenn Herr POHL heute behauptet, dass er das nicht gewusst hat, dann hat

es der Rottenfuehrer MEIER gewusst.

.Fr. Wie werten Sie POHL?

A. Ich habe keine Lust mehr in den Court zu gehen. POHL war sicher ein sehr

aktiver Mann, vielleicht ein Werkzeug HIMMLER'S.

57.Fr. Die Frage ist nicht ganz so klar, wenn man die Frage zerlegt, dass POHL der Traeger des Gedankens des Arbeitseinsatzes war und so kann man sich doch nicht erklaeren, dass Leute vernichtet wurden im Sinne des Arbeitseinsatzes

A. Aber die, die nicht arbeiten konnten, was ist mit den Kindern und Muettern

58.Fr. Dem kann man gegenueberstellen, dass Kinder gearbeitet haben und dass Leute gearbeitet haben, die nicht mehr arbeitseinsatzfaehig waren. Dass POHL davon gewusst hat, ist kein Zweifel. Mich wuerde Ihre Einschaetzung interessieren, dass POHL ein Exponent der Vernichtungsidee war oder die Leute zu Tode arbeiten liess.

174

A. Ich zaehle POHL nicht zu dem Kreis der Manner, die dieses Vernichtungswerk gegen die Juden geboren hat. Ich beurteile POHL als einen sehr eitlen, herrschsuechtigen und einflusshungrigen Mann. Statt dass der zu HIMMLER gesagt hat, nein, das kann ich nicht machen, sagte er immer, ja das kann man machen, also ein"Jasager."

59.Fr. Was ist Ihre persoenliche Meinung. Ist dieser Vernichtung ein formeller Beschluss vorangegangen?

A. Alles das, was ich sage ist nicht ein Wissen.

60.Fr. Nun Ihre persoenliche Meinung?

A. Dem muss ein Beschluss vorangegangen sein.

61.Fr. Wie entwickelt?

A. Entwickelt hat sich die Sache bestimmt. Es hat mal der Plan "Madagaskar" bestanden. Damals hat man oeffentlich noch nicht an eine Vernichtung gedacht, aber wie man heute aus den Protokollen liest, laeuft die Sache seit 1942.

62.Fr. Wer hat einen solchen Beschluss gefasst, oder welches Kremium ist zustaendig?

A.   Dr.MORGEN, der Ihnen ein Begriff ist, hat behauptet, dass die Dinge in der

Kanzlei des Fuehrers geboren wurden.

3.Fr. Obwohl er gar keine Moeglichkeit hat, das zu wissen.

A.   Dieser kombiniert ja ueberhaupt.

4.Fr. GOERING?

A.   GOERING, GOEBBELS steht in Frage, wogegen HITLER, ROSENBERG, FRANK alles

Leute waeren, die dafuer in Frage kaemen. Aber ich kann darueber nichts

Genaues sagen.

5.Fr. Die Frage ist nur von historischer Bedeutung.

A.   Selbstverstaendlich, aber ich kann darueber nichts sagen. Ich bin nur der

Meinung, dass eben HIMMLER das Werkzeug gestellt hat, wahrscheinlich auch

mit vollem Wollen gestellt hat. Er hat aber mit Ausnahme von einem eng um-   175

gfenztem Kreis, die es gemacht und gewusst haben, gearbeitet und die Milli-

onen SS-Maenner, von denen der weitaus groesste Teil zu Unrecht in diese

Belastung hereingezogen werden -

.Fr. Ich glaube Sie machen einen Fehler. Der Kreis war wesentlich groesser.

A.   Sehen Sie mal, bei einer Million waere ein kleiner Kreis 10 Tausend.

.Fr. Ich moechte Ihnen ein Beispiel sagen. 1 x hat davon gewusst ein Grossteil

der ganzen Hauptaemter der SS, dann die oertliche Dienststelle z.B. Ausch-

witz; ueber Auschwitz war eine staendige Rauchwolke, und es gab keine Zi-

vilperson, die nicht gewusst hat, was los ist, also mal die ganze Bevoel-

kerung hat das gewusst. Es haben ferner gewusst die Stellen der Reichsbahn,

die die Transporte geleitet haben, die Leute, die gebaut haben, die Inge-

nieure, die die Plaene entworfen haben, die I.G.Farben, die das Gas dazu

geliefert hat usw.usw.. Und da fragen Sie, wie gross der Kreis war.

A. Die reinen Soldaten haben es nicht gewusst. Ich war 3 Jahre an der Front als Offizier und als Mann und da kann ich sagen, dass es die Maenner nicht gewusst haben. Ich weiss nicht, ob Herr Dr.KASTNER sich daran erinnert, als zuerst zwischen Dr.KASTNER, BILLITZ und mir gesprochen wurde, dass ich Auschwitz nicht einmal dem Namen nach gekannt habe. Auf der Karte, die in meinem Zimmer gehaengt ist, habe ich den Ort erst suchen muessen.

68.Fr. Herr BECHER dagegen spricht eine einzige Tatsache. In Budapest haben Sie eine Reihe von Juden mit den sogenannten Schutzbriefen beschenkt. Sie sind zu intellegent, um sich nicht die Frage zu stellen, woher diese Todesangst stammt.

A. Ja, ich erklaere Ihnen, in den ersten Tagen als ich in Budapest war, wartete ich auf eine Besprechung mit Herrn KALTENBRUNNER. Ich wollte eine Unterstuetzung bei Herrn VEESEMAYER wegen der Pferde. Erinnern Sie sich an das Hotel Astoria? In dem Moment ist mir zum 1.Mal klar geworden, um Gottes Willen, was passiert denn da. Da kamen Menschen herein, wir standen in der frueheren Bar und ich habe zu WELISCH gesagt, wir warten vor der Tuer und warten ab, was da los ist. Als Deutscher sagte ich, was wird hier gespielt; ohne zu wissen, dass Leute vergast wurden, allein schon die Todesangst, die die Leute hatten, veranlasste mich ihnen einen Schutzbrief zu geben. Dass diese Leute alle um ihr Leben gekaempft haben, darueber war ich mir in kurzer Zeit klar; sonst haette ich nicht alle diese Dinge angestrebt. Das ganze Lastwagenspiel war wirklich ein Spiel und dass ich Mitte August diese Sache weitergemacht habe und HIMMLER gegenueber gespielt habe, das habe ich nicht getan als Verraeter an Deutschland und Betrueger an HIMMLER, sondern als Deutscher und ich habe gesagt, hier muss ich das

176

A.   tun, da HITLER nicht Deutschland war. Das muessen Sie glauben, dass ich

      davon ueberzeugt war.

9.Fr. Wir muessen unterbrechen. Herr BECHER ich will Ihnen noch sagen, dass Sie

      Ihre persoenlichen Fragen noch an Herrn Dr.KASTNER stellen koennen.

- - - - - - - -

177

Ka.

STAFF EVIDENCE ANALYSIS   By: Ernst A. Schlomann
                                 Date: 4 June 1948

DOCUMENT NO: NID-15533

Title and/or general nature: Affidavit by Albert THOMS
                                 re: 76 deliveries of valuab-
                                 les made by SS to German
                                 Reichsbank under the name of
                                 Melmer. A part of these ship-
                                 ments consisting of gold,
                                 foreign exchange, jewelry,
                                 precious stones, pearls,
                                 crowns for teeth and fillings
                                 which could not be worked on
                                 and sorted any more were sent
                                 to the salt mines in Merkers
                                 in their original containers,
                                 i.e. boxes, packages, trunks
                                 and other containers.

Doc. 9

178

Date: 26 May 1948

Source (Location of
        original, etc):   OCCWC Document Room,Nurnberg
                                 Transmitted by the American
                                 authorities in charge of
                                 Reichsbank Frankfurt.
Persons, firms or organi-
zations involved: PUHL, Emil

To be filed under these
reference headings: NID - PUHL, Emil

SUMMARY :   contents: see title above

- 1 -
"END"

<u>Erklaerung unter Eid</u>

Ich, Albert Thoms, nachdem ich darauf aufmerksam gemacht worden bin, dass ich mich wegen falscher Aussage strafbar mache, stelle hiermit unter Eid und ohne Zwang freiwillig folgendes fest:

Waehrend meiner Amtszeit in Berlin bei der Deutschen Reichsbank wurden von der SS insgesamt 76 Ablieferungen von Wertgegenstaenden gemacht, die unter dem Namen Melmer gefuehrt wurden. Ich habe diese Ablieferungen bereits anderwaerts in einer Eidesstattlichen Erklaerung und in meiner Aussage vor dem Internationalen Militaertribunal in Nuernberg am 15. 5. 1946 beschrieben. Von diesen 76 Ablieferungen gelangte ein Teil nicht mehr zur Verwertung, da durch die Kriegsumstaende die Wertgegenstaende der Reichsbank (Gold etc.) evakuiert und in Sicherheit gebracht wurden. Die Gesamtverlagerung wurde in das Quittungsbuch der Edelmetall-Ankaufskasse der Reichsbank auf speziell rot numerierten Seiten 1 - 15 eingetragen. Ich erkenne die beigeschlossenen Photokopien als korrekte Kopien der Seiten 14 und 15 dieses Buches an. Die uebriggebliebenen Melmer Lieferungen, insgesamt 207 Behaelter, die ebenfalls verlagert wurden, setzten sich aus Gold, Devisen, Schmuckgegenstaenden, Edelsteinen, Perlen, (ausgebrochenen) Zahnkronen und Zahnersatz zusammen. Da diese Lieferungen nicht mehr bearbeitet und sortiert werden konnten, wurden sie in den Originalbehaeltern, Kisten, Paketen, Koffern und anderen Behaeltern nach den Salzbergwerken in Merkers verbracht.

Ich habe die obige Erklaerung, bestehend aus einer Seite, sorgfaeltig durchgelesen, habe die notwendigen Korrekturen in meiner eigenen Handschrift gemacht und habe sie abgezeichnet und erklaere hiermit unter Eid, dass ich nach bestem Wissen und Gewissen die reine Wahrheit gesagt habe.

Albert Thoms

ALBERT THOMS
Signed and sworn to before me this 26th day of May 1948 at Frankfurt, Germany, by Albert Thoms, known to me to be the person making the above affidavit.

179

A F F I D A V I T

I, Albert THOMS, having been warned that I will be liable for punishment for making false statements, herewith state voluntarily and without coercion under oath the following:

During my term of office in Berlin with the German Reichsbank, in toto 76 deliveries of valuables were made by the SS which were listed under the name "MELMER". I had already described these deliveries in an affidavit, and also in my testimony before the International Military Tribunal in Nuremberg on 15 May 1946. Of these 76 deliveries, a part was not utilized anymore, since due to conditions of war, the valuables of the Reichsbank (gold, etc.) were evacuated and brought to a safe place. The entire shifting was entered into the receipt book of the purcha-sing office for precious metals of the Reichsbank on special red-numbered pages 1/15. I acknowledge the enclosed photocopies to be correct copies of the pages 14 and 15 of this book. The remaining MELMER deliveries, in toto 207 containers which were also shifted, were composed of gold, foreign exchange, jewelry, precious stones, pearls, crowns for teeth and fillings. Since these deliveries could not be processed and sort-ed anymore, they were brought to the salt mines in Merkers in the original containers, i.e. boxes, packages, trunks, and other containers.

I have carefully read the above declaration, consisting of one page, have made the necessary corrections in my own handwriting, and have initialed them. I state herewith under oath that the above is the pure truth according to my best knowledge and belief.

signed: ALBERT THOMS

Signed and sworn to before me this 26th day of May 1948 at Frankfurt, Germany, by Albert THOMS, known to me to be the person making the above affidavit.

signed: OTTO VERBER
U.S.Civ. A-444385
OCCWC APO 696-A

CERTIFICATE OF TRANSLATION

I, Ernst A. Schlomann, hereby certify that I am thoroughly conversant with the English and German languages and that the above is a true and correct translation of Document No. NID-15533

8 June 1948

sign.: ERNST A. SCHLOMANN
Research Analyst
AGO # D-047668

180

Ka.   OFFICE OF CHIEF OF COUNSEL
                FOR WAR CRIMES
        APO 696-A   U.S. ARMY

STAFF EVIDENCE ANALYSIS   By: Ernst A. Schlomann
                               Date: 4 June 1948

Document No.:   NID-15534

Title and/or general nature: Photostatic copy of list of
                               dental gold and silver items
                               sent by THOMS and (illegible)
                               of Deutsche Reichsbank Haupt-
                               kasse to Preussische Staats-
                               muenze (Government mint)
                               with the request to melt them
                               down and assay then.

Source (Location of original,
        etc.):   OCCWC Document Room Nurnberg
                               Transmitted by the American
                               authorities in charge of
Persons, firms or organi-   Reichsbank Frankfurt
zations involved: PUHL, Emil'   *Doc. 10*
                               Reichsbank, Berlin
                                                               181

To be filed under these
reference headings: NID - PUHL, Emil

SUMMARY (Indicate page numbers): contents: see title above

Entwurf   Reinschrift ausgehändi

Berlin, den 24.11.44.

Hauptkasse

Gef. Ne
Gel.
Ab m. Anl.
24 XI 1944

An die

Preussische Staatsmünze

Berlin

182

Betr.: 46.Lieferung (M)   24.11.1944

Wir übersenden Ihnen anbei:

		kgr	kgbrutto	Btl.Nr
378	Nr.1/1: Zahnersatz Weissmetall	4,370.0	5,647	1
	/4: Dublee	1,206.0		
379	Nr.1/1: Zahnersatz Gold	0,156.0	5,043	2
	/4: Gold	4,817.0		
380	Nr.2/1: Silber	28,591.0	28,855	4
381	Nr.4/1: Gold	25,157	25,373	7
	Dublee			
	/2: Zahnersatz Gold			
	" Weissmetall			
382	Nr.5/1: Silber	22,950	23,385	8
383	"	21,235	21,503	9
384	"	17,633	17,910	10

mit der Bitte um Einschmelzung und
Probierung.   Deutsche Reichsbank
              Hauptkasse

STAFF EVIDENCE ANALYSIS, Ministries Division.

By: Schoenfeldt.
Date: 16 December 1947.

Document Number:	NG-4096.
Title and/or general nature:	Letter from the SS Wirtschafts-Verwaltungshauptamt (SS economic and administrative main office) to SCHWERIN-KROSIGK concerning the confiscated property of Jews.
Form of Document:	Typescript.
Stamps and other endorsements:	"Secret". Signed by an SS-Obergruppenfuehrer, probably Pohl. notes by PATZER.
Date:	24 July 1944.
Source:	Archives of the former Finance Ministry, Bln.-Charlottenburg (OCC-BBT 6054).

Doc. 11

183

PERSONS OR ORGANIZATIONS IMPLICATED:

SCHWERIN-KROSIGK
PATZER

TO BE FILED UNDER THESE REFERENCE HEADINGS:

NG-Finance Ministry

SUMMARY:

This letter is the answer to a letter from SCHWERIN-KROSIGK, and concerns the confiscated property of Jews taken to concentration camps. Currency, foreign money, securities, jewelery and articles of rare metals are in question. The letter constitutes: "The values go to the concentration camps." Details are given on how to convert the jewelery and so on into money. The proceeds are to be credited to an account of the Finance Ministry. Marking of this account: "Max HEILIGER". (Max Saint.).

- END -

184

Reichsfinanzministerium, Abt. Gen. B.

Gruppe: _____

Ref. Patzer

Inhalt: _____

Gen. B. / 5

Vom _19. 4. 1941_ bis ____ ____ 19 ____

Band _1_   Fortf. Band _____

Vorakten: ____

Sammelakte

Standort:

Zimmer Nr. _337_

Hirmann

Geheim!

Abschrift zu O 5400 - 32/44 VI

Der Chef
des SS-Wirtschafts-Verwaltungshauptamts

A II/3 Reinh./Ka/Ro Geh.Tgb.Nr.66/44

Berlin, den 24.7.1944
Lichterfelde-West
Unter den Eichen 126-135

Betr. Beschlagnahmtes Judenvermögen
Bezug: Dortiges Schreiben vom 15.7.44 Az.O 5221 A - 225 VI

An den

Herrn Reichsminister der
Finanzen
Berlin W 8
Wilhelmplatz 1/2

Zu obigem Schreiben wird mitgeteilt :

Es handelt sich um Judenwerte, die zugunsten des Reiches einge-
zogen sind, und zwar

Reichsmarkbeträge,
RKK-Scheine,
Devisen in Münzen und Noten,
Wertpapiere sowie
Schmuckstücke und Gebrauchsgegenstände aus Edel-
metallen aller Art.

Die Beifügung einer Aufstellung ist wegen des zu grossen Umfanges
nicht möglich. Die Werte fallen in Konzentrationslagern an.

Es wird darauf hingewiesen, dass in dieser Angelegenheit bereits
mehrfach Besprechungen mit einem Beauftragten des RFM. stattgefunden haben. Die letzte Besprechung hat am 11.5.43 zwischen SS-
Gruppenführer und Generalleutnant der Waffen-SS F r a n k und
Herrn Regierungsdirektor P a t z e r stattgefunden.

Die Verwertung wird wie folgt durchgeführt :

Geldsorten aller Art sowie Wertpapiere werden durch die Reichs-
hauptbank, Abt. Edelmetalle - Bankrat T h o m s - bearbeitet.
Schmuck- und Gebrauchsgegenstände aus Edelmetallen werden durch
die Städtische Pfandleihanstalt, Abteilung 3, Zentralstelle,
Berlin N 4, - Amtsrat W i e s e r - verwertet.

In einer am 24.7.44 durchgeführten Besprechung beim Beauftragten für den Vierjahresplan wurde Übereinstimmung über
die weitere beschleunigte Bearbeitung der angefallenen Werte
erzielt.

Die Erlöse werden an die Reichshauptkasse zugunsten Reichsfinanzministerium, Sonderkonto "Max Heiliger", überwiesen.

Auf

185

Auf diesbezügliche hiesige Mitteilung an den Rechnungshof des
Deutschen Reiches, nachrichtlich an RFM, vom 19.11.43 - Az.
A II/3 Reinh.Geh.Tgb.Nr.1-2/43, dertiges Az. J 7070-89 I,
wird Bezug genommen.

                              Unterschrift

                              ϟϟ-Obergruppenführer und
                              General der Waffen - ϟϟ

                         - - - - - -

186

By: Walter Speyer
Date: 21 February 1948

STAFF EVIDENCE ANALYSIS, Ministries Division

Document Number: NG-4983

Title and/or general nature: Affidavit of Peter MELMER,
                             SS-Hauptsturmfuehrer and
                             Chief of the pay-office of
                             the WV-Hauptamt on delivery
                             of values from the con-
                             centration-camps to the
                             Reichsbank at the disposal
                             of the Ministry of Finance.

Form of Document: Typed original.

Stamps and other endorsements:

                             signed.

Date: 11 February 48

Source: OCCWC Doc. Centre.

PERSONS OR ORGANIZATIONS IMPLICATED: *Doc. 12*

                             SCHWERIN-KROSIGK
                             POHL   **187**
                             FRANK
                             MELMER

TO BE FILED UNDER THESE REFERENCE HEADINGS:

                    NG — Reich Ministry of Finance
                         NG — Concentration Camps.

SUMMARY: See title.

END

EIDESSTATTLICHE ERKLAERUNG.

Ich, Bruno, August, Hermann, Peter MELMER, SS-Hauptsturmfuehrer und Leiter der
Amtskasse des WV-Hauptamtes, schwoere, sage aus und erklaere:

1. Etwa im Mai 1942 erhielt ich von dem Chef des WV-Hauptamtes, SS-Obergruppenfuehrer POHL, den Auftrag, beschlagnahmte Werte aus den Konzentrationslagern,
   die in Berlin bei mir abgeliefert werden, an die Reichsbank Berlin, Abteilung
   Edelmetalle, bei Herrn THOMS abzuliefern. Fuer die Ablage des Schriftwechsels
   bestimmte Obergruppenfuehrer FRANK, dass die Akten die Bezeichnung "REINHARDT"
   tragen sollten. Herr POHL hat mir mitgeteilt, dass in einer Besprechung mit
   der Reichsbank das Abrechnungsverfahren derart geklaert sei, dass die abgelieferten Werte zu Gunsten des Reiches verwertet und der Gegenwert auf ein noch
   naeher zu bestimmendes Konto bei der Reichshauptkasse zur Verfuegung des Reichsfinanzministeriums ueberwiesen werden sollte.

188

2. Obergruppenfuehrer FRANK hat mir dann etwa im Sommer 1942 mitgeteilt, dass
   die Kontobezeichnung bei der Reichshauptkasse "Max HEILIGER" lautet. Die Ablieferung an die Reichsbank erfolgte von der zweiten Sendung ab in plombierten,
   bzw. versiegelten Behaeltern. Ich erhielt von der Reichsbank eine Quittung
   unter auf dem Durchschlag des Inhaltsverzeichnisses mit dem Text: Vorstehend
   versiegelte und plombierte Behaelter mit dem angeblich oben angegebenen Inhalt
   vorbehaltlich der Nachpruefung durch die Reichsbank richtig uebernommen. Nach
   einiger Zeit erhielt ich in regelmaessigen Abstaenden Abrechnungen der Reichsbank ueber die abgelieferten Werte. Die Abrechnung schloss mit dem Vermerk,
   dass der angegebene Gegenwert in Reichsmark auf das genannte Konto bei der
   Reichshauptkasse zur Verfuegung des Reichsfinanzministeriums ueberwiesen sei,
   d.h., dass der Erloes aus der Verwertung der Devisen, des angefallenen Schmuckes
   und der Edelmetalle in Reichsmark an das Finanzministerium gezahlt wurde.

Diese Aussagen habe ich freiwillig gemacht, ohne jedwedes Versprechen auf Belch-
nung und ich war keinerlei Zwang oder Druck ausgesetzt. Ich habe diese Erklaerung
sorgfaeltig durchgelesen und eigenhaendig gegengezeichnet, habe die notwendigen

NG - 4983
- 2 -

Korrekturen vorgenommen und mit meinen Anfängsbuchstaben gegengezeichnet und erklaere hiermit unter Eid, dass alle die von mir in dieser EIDESSTATTLICHEN ERKLAE-
RUNG angegebenen Tatsachen nach meinem besten Wissen und Gewissen der vollen Wahrheit entsprechen.

Nuernberg, den 11. Februar 1948.

_____
Bruno August Hermann Peter MELMER

Before me, Larry L. WOLFF, US-Civilian, AGO indentification number A-442665,
Interrogator, Evidence Division, Office of Chief of Counsel for War Crimes
appeared Bruno August Hermann Peter MELMER to me known, who in my presence
signed the foregoing statement (Erklaerung) consisting of two (2) pages in the
German language and swere that the same was true on the 11th day of February 1948.

189

_____
signature (Larry L. WOLFF)

_ End -

DECLARATION IN LIEU OF OATH

I, Bruno, August, Hermann, Peter MELMER, SS-Hauptsturmfuehrer and chief of the pay-office of the WV-Main office
take the oath and declare:

1)   Approximately in May 1942 I got the order by the chief of
the WV-Main-office, SS-Obergruppenfuehrer POHL, to hand over
confiscated values from the concentration-camps which had
been delivered to me in Berlin, to the Reichsbank Berlin,
department "precious metals", to Herrn THOMS. Obergruppenfuehrer FRANK ordered, with regard to the filing of the correspondence, that the documents should be marked "REINHARDT".
Herr POHL informed me that in a discussion with the Reichsbank the procedure of balancing of accounts was clarified
in that way that the values which were handed over should
be realized in favour of the Reich and the equivalent should
be transferred to an account still to be fixed with the Reich
main-pay-office to the disposal of the Reich Finance Ministry.

2)   Obergruppenfuehrer FRANK then informed me circa in
summer 1942 that the account with the Reich main-pay-office
is marked: "Max Heiliger". The delivery to the Reichsbank
took place in sealed containers or in containers sealed with
lead from the second sending onward. I received from the Reichsbank a receipt on the copy of the table of contents with the
words: Enclosed sealed containers with the supposed contents
stated above duly taken over by the Reichsbank on condition
of verification. After some times I received in regular
intervals settlements of accounts of the Reichsbank on the
delivered values. The settlement of account ended with the
note that the stated equivalent in Reichsmark was transferred
to the named account with the Reich main cash office to the
disposal of the Reich Ministry of Finance, that means that
the proceeds from the realization of the foreign currency,

- 1 -

190

the forfeited Jewellery and the precious metals were paid in
Reichsmark to the Ministry of Finance.

This statement I have made voluntarily, without any
promise of reward and I was under no coercion or pressure.
I have read through this declaration carefully and signed it
with my own signature, I have made the necessary

(page 2 of original)

corrections and countersigned them with my initals and I herewith declare under oath that all the facts stated by me in
this declaration on lieu of oath are absolutely true to the
best of my conscience.

Nuremberg, the 11 February 1948

signed: Bruno MELMER

191

Before me, Larry L. WOLFF, US-Civilian, AGO indentification
number A-442665, Interrogator, Evidence Division, Office of
Chief of Counsel for War Crimes appeared Bruno August Hermann
Peter MELMER to me known, who in my presence signed the foregoing statement (Erklaerung) consisting of two (2) pages in
the German language and swore that the same was true on the
11th day of February 1948

signed: Larry L. WOLFF

CERTIFICATE OF TRANSLATION

I, Walter SPEYER, Allied Civilian No. 20194, hereby certify
that I am thoroughly conversant with the English and German
languages and the above is a true and correct translation
of the sworn affidavit of Bruno, August, Hermann, Peter MELMER
of 11th February 1948.

Nuremberg, 26 February 1948   Walter SPEYER

"END"

STAFF EVIDENCE ANALYSIS, Criminal Organizations   By: Mr. M. Wolfson
                                                         Date: 10 July 1946

Doc. No. or other description: NO-061

Title and/or general nature: Detailed Inventory report by Globocnik
                                        on Value of Goods Seized During
                                        "Acción Reinhardt"

Date: 27 February 1943

Source (Location of original, etc):   PFSS Files Berlin Document Center
                                        (BDC) File No. IV red folder "KL
                                        und Wacheinheiten" 4 pages

Language of original.   German

PERSONS OR ORGANIZATIONS IMPLICATED: SS Sturmbannführer Wippern
                                        SS Obergruppenführer Pohl
                                        SS Gruppenführer Globocnik

Doc. 13

192

TO BE FILED UNDER THESE REFERENCE HEADINGS: NO- SS WVHA
                                            NO- Deportation of human beings
                                            NO- Spoliation of Foreign Property
                                            NO- Concentration Camps
                                            NO- Forced Labor
                                            NO- SS, General
                                            NO- Persons as above
                                            NI- General

SUMMARY: (Indicate page nos. of original or translation):

        This is the detailed list referred to in NO-060 entitled List of
valuable Jewish properties which have been delivered prior to 3 February 1943.
        It is written up and signed by SS Sturmbannführer Wippern, director of
Administration.
        The main groups of this list are:
                1) Cash delivered to SS WVHA   RM   53,013,133.51
                2) Foreign currency in bills   RM   1,452,904.65
                3) Foreign currency in gold coins   RM   843,802.75
                4) Valuable metals   RM   5,353,943.00
                5) Miscellaneous valuable goods   RM   26,089,800.00
                6) Clothes, materials   RM   13,294,400.00
                                         Totaling   RM   100,047,983.91

See NO-056, NO-057, NO-058, NO-059, NO-060, NO-062, NO-063, NO-064

wertmäßige Aufstellung der bis zum 3.2.1943 zur Ablieferung
gelangten Judensachen.

1.) Kassenbestände: RM 15.931.722,o1
    Ablieferung #-Wirtsch. Krakau   "   31.500.000,—
    #-W.-V.Hauptamt Berlin (R.B.)   "   5.581.411,50
                                             RM 53.013.133,51

2.) Devisen in Noten: Kurs:
    USA Dollar   505.046,—   2,50   RM   1.262.615,—
    Pal. £   1.069,—   9.3o   "   9.941,7o
    Pengö   16.435   —.6o   "   9.861,—
    Rubel   294.070,—   —.1o   "   29.407,—
    Engl. £   3.822.-/-   9.3o   "   35.544,6o
    Canad.Dollar   3.840,75   2.5o   "   9.601,87
    Pesetas   131.-   2.4o   "   314,4o
    Kc.   789.630.-   —.1o   "   78.963,—
    Ffrs.   22.767.5o   —.o5   "   1.138,37
    Brasil.Frs.   8.-   —.o9   "   —.72
    Südafr. £   28 ^{1o}/- 4.4o   "   125,4o
    Türk. £   5.5o   1.9o   "   1o,45
    Holl.Gulden   1.72o,—   1.33   "   2.287,6o
    Schweiz.Frs   7.53o.-   5.8o   "   4.367,4o
    Lire   883.-   —.13   "   114,79
    Lewa   1oo.-   —.o1   "   1,—
    Austral. £   15 ^{1o}/- 2.5o   "   38,75
    Lei   13.486.-   —.o2   "   269,72
    Ägyp. £   4 ^{1o}/- 4.4o   "   19,8o
    Belga   4.2o3.-   —.4o   "   1.681,2o
    Lats   1o.-   —.1o   "   1,—
    Argent. Pesos   9o.-   1.-   "   9o,—
    Paragu.   1o.-   —.6o   "   6,—
    Schwed. Kr.   455.-   —.6o   "   273,—
    Norw. Kr.   165.-   —.6o   "   99,—
    Dinare   3o.-   —.o5   "   1,5o
    Karbowanek   1.555.-   —.1o   "   155,5o
    Slow.Kronen   59.6o8.75   —.1o   "   5.96o,88
    Litas   14o.-   —.1o   "   14,—
                                             RM   1.452.9o4,65

                                                         - 2 -

3.) Devisen in ermixten Gold: Kurs

USA Dollar	116.425.–	4.20	RM	488.985,–
Rubel	91.362.–	2.15	"	196.428,30
Engl. L	3.822.–	20.40	"	77.969,–
Öst. Kronen	30.940.–	–.85	"	26.299,–
Öst. Schilling	1.975.–		"	1.185,–
Dukaten	2.366.–	10.–	"	23.660,–
Fin.Mark	20.–	1.–	"	20,–
Reicgsmark	12.730.–	1.–	"	12.730,–
Zloty	1.080.–	–.50		540,–
Dän.Kronen	230.–	–.52	"	119,60
Cech.Dukaten	2.–	10.–	"	20,–
Port.Reis	15.000.–(150 Esc)	1.–	"	150,–
Pesetas	25.–	1.50	"	37.50
Franz.Frs.	8.005.–	1.62		12.968,10
Südafr.L	2.–	20.40	"	40,80
Türk. L	47.–	3.50	"	164,50
Holl.Gulden	315.–	17.–(f.10 fl.)	"	535,50
Schweiz.Frs.	490.–	16.50(f.20 Frs.)	"	404,25
Lire	1.210.–	–.50		605,–
Austr.L	10.–	20.40	"	172,60
Lei	1.140.–	–.50	"	570,–
Belga	140.–	–.50	"	70,–
Schwed.Kr.	20.–	11.20(f.10 Kr.)	"	22,40
Norw.Kr.	35.–	11.20(f.10 Kr.)	"	39,20
Dinare	30.–	–.50	"	15,–
Cuban.Pesos	10.–	4.20	"	42,–
Alb.Frs.	20.–	.50	"	10,–
			RM	843.802,75

4.) Edelmetalle:

1.775,46 kg Gold in Barren à RM 2.784.–		RM	4.942.870,–
9.639,– kg Silber à " 40.–		"	385.573,–
5,10 kg Bruchsilber à " 5.000.–		"	25.500,–
		RM	5.353.943,–

) Sonstige Werte:

			à RM		RM	
5 St.	Drehbleistifte gold		à RM	30.-	RM	150,--
17 "	Füllhalter "		à "	70,-	"	1.190,--
4 "	Damenplatinuhren		à "	300,-	"	1.200,--
2894 "	Herrentaschenuhren gold		à "	500,-	"	1.427.000,--
578 "	Herrenarmbanduhren "		à "	300,-	"	173.400,--
7313 "	Damenarmbanduhren "		à "	250,-	"	1.828.250,--
19 "	Platinuhrengehäuse m.Brill.u. Diamanten		à "	1000,-	"	19.000,--
280 "	Armbänder m.Brill.u.Diam.		à "	3500,-	"	980.000,--
6245 "	Herrenarmbanduhren		à "	10,-	"	62.450,--
13455 "	Herrentaschenuhren		à "	20,-	"	269.100,--
1 "	Herrentaschenuhr gold m.Brill.		à "	600,-	"	600,--
179 "	Damengolduhren m.Brill.u.Diam.		à "	600.-	"	107.400,--
7 "	Damenringuhren gold		à "	150.-	"	1.050,--
4 "	Damenhängeuhren m. Perlen		à "	200,-	"	800,--
394 "	Damenhängeuhren m.Brill.		à "	600,-	"	236.400,--
228 "	Damenplatinbrillantuhren		à "	1200.-	"	273.600,--
293 "	Damenhängeuhren gold		à "	250.-	"	73.250,--
22324 "	Brillen		à "	3.-	"	66.972,--
3 Paar	Manschettenknöpfe m.Brill.		à "	150.-	"	450,--
11675 St.	Ringe aus Gold m.Brill.u.Diam.		à "	1500.-	"	11.675.000,--
7200 "	Damenarmbanduhren		à "	10.-	"	72.000,--
40 "	Goldbroschen		à "	350.-	"	14.000,--
1399 Paar	Ohrringe aus gold m.Brill.		à "	250.-	"	349.750.--
169 St.	Anstecknadeln m.Brill.u.Diam.		à "	100.-	"	16.900,--
1974 "	Broschen aus Gold "		à "	2000.-	"	3.948.000,--
27 "	Armreifen "		à "	250.-	"	6.750,--
49 kg	Perlen				"	4.000.000,--
7000 St.	Füllhalte		à "	10,-	"	70.000,--
150 "	einzelne große Brillanten		à "	1000.-	"	150.000,--
2 "	Halsketten m. Brill.u.Diamanten		"	1500.-	"	3.000,--
1 "	goldenes Zigarettenetui		à "	400.-	"	400,--
1 "	Perlmutterkästchen				"	20,--
3 S	Puderdosen in Gold		à "	50,-	"	150,--
2	Operngläser aus Perlmutter		à "	50.-	"	100,--
1,44 kg	Korallen				"	150,--
51370 St.	Reparaturuhren			3.-		256.850,--
1000 "	Drehbleistifte		à "	3.-	"	3.000,--
350 "	Rasierapparate		à "	2.50	"	875,--
800 S	Taschenmesser		à "	1.-	"	800,--
32 0	Geldbörsen		à "	1.50	"	44.850,--

195

315 St.	Brieftaschen	à	à RM	2,50	RM	1.537,50
1500 "	Scheren	à "	-,50	"	750,—
230 "	Taschenlampen	à "	-,50	"	115,—
2554 "	Reparaturwecker	à "	3,—	"	7.662,—
160 "	Wecker gangbar	à "	6,—	"	960,—
477 "	Sonnenbrillen	à "	-,50	"	238,50
41 "	silberne Zigarettendosen"	30,—	"	1.230,—
230 "	Fieberthermometer	à "	3,—	"	690,—

RM 26.089.800,—

6.) Spinnstoffe:

462 Waggon	Lumpen	à "	700,—	RM	323.400,—
251 "	Bettfedern	à "	10.000,—	"	2.510.000,—
317 "	Bekleidung u.Wäsche	à "	33.000,—	"	10.461.000,—

RM 13.294.400,—

Z u s a m m e n s t e l l u n g

1. Abgeliefertes Bargeld u.Barbestand	RM	53.013.133,51
2. Devisen in Noten	RM	1.452.904,65
3. Devisen in gemünztem Gold	RM	843.802,75
4. Edelmetalle	RM	5.353.943,—
5. Sonstiges	RM	26.089.800,—
6. Spinnstoffe	RM	13.294.400,—

RM 100.047.983,91

-Sturmbannführer.

Lublin, den 27. Februar 1943

CJ

COPY . Secret

B / Ch 186

Personal staff of the
Reichsfuehrer-SS
Administration
of Central Files
File No. Secret

REPORT

6 February 1943

on the realization of textile-salvage from the Jewish resettlement
up to the present date.

The enclosed statement gives an account of the quantity of old garments
from the Jewish resettlement, that has been sent from the camps of
Auschwitz and Lublin up to the present date. In this connection special
consideration must be given to the fact that the delivery of rags is very
high. As a result, the amount of usable old garments, especially men's
clothing, is naturally diminished. It has therefore not been possible
to satisfy the demand for men's clothing to its full.

The transportation by rail proved to be especially difficult. Through
the continually recurring transportation stoppages, the dispatch was held
up with the resulting in temporary accumulations in the individual
camps.

The transportation hold-up to the Ukraine has been especially noticeable
since December 1942, and prevented the delivery of old clothing intended
for the racial Germans there. The whole delivery to the racial Germans
in the Ukraine was, therefore, taken by the office for Germanization
to Litzmannstadt and there placed in a large store. As soon as the
transportation situation is relieved, the inner-office for Germanization
will carry out the distribution.

Up till now the supply of the great amount of necessary cars has been
carried out in close co-operation with and through the Reich Ministry
for Economics. Also, in future, the Reich Ministry for Economics will
endeavour to obtain cars for the dispatch of old materials from the
Government General through the Reich Ministry for Transportation, making
reference to the bad situation in respect of textile raw materials.

sign. POHL

SS-Obergruppenfuehrer and
General of the Waffen-SS

Certified true copy:

(Signature) KERSTEN

SS-Hauptsturmfuehrer

Doc. 14

197

- 1 -

COPY. Secret

STATEMENT

Personal staff of the
Reichsfuehrer-SS
Administration of Central
Files
File No. Secret 181/6

on the quantities of old textile-materials delivered from the camps of
Lublin and Auschwitz by order of the SS Economic & Administrative Main
Office.

1. Reich Ministry of Economics

Men's old clothing without underwear   97.000 sets
Women's old clothing without underwear   76.000 sets
Women's silk underwear   89.000 sets

                                     total: 34 cars

Rags	400 cars	2.700.000 kg
Bed-feathers	130 cars	270.000 kg
women's hair	1 car	3.000 kg
scrap material	5 cars	19.000 kg
total:		2.992.000 kg

                                     total   536 cars

                                                  570 cars

198

2. Office for Germanization.

Men's clothing:			Children's clothing	
Overcoats	99.000		overcoats	15.000
jackets	57.000		boy's jackets	11.000
vests	27.000		boys' pants	3.000
pants	62.000		shirts	3.000
drawers	38.000		scarves	4.000
shirts	132.000		pullovers	1.000
pullovers	9.000		drawers	1.000
scarves	2.000		girls' dresses	9.000
pyjamas	6.000		girls' chemises	5.000
collars	10.000		aprons	2.000
gloves	2.000	pairs	drawers	5.000
socks	10.000	"	stockings	10.000 pairs
shoes	31.000	"	shoes	22.000 "

Women's clothing			Linen etc.	
coats	155.000	pieces	bed covers	37.000 pieces
dresses	119.000	"	bed sheets	46.000 "
jackets	26.000	"	pillow slips	75.000 "
shirts	30.000	"	tea towels	27.000 "
chemises	125.000	"	handkerchiefs	135.000 "
blouses	30.000	"	hand towels	100.000 "
pullovers	60.000	"	table cloths	11.000 "
drawers	49.000	"	napkins	8.000 "
panties	60.000	"	woollen shawls	6.000 "
pyjamas	27.000	"	ties	
aprons	36.000	"	rubber shoes	
brassieres	25.000	"	and boots	24.000 pairs
underwear	22.000	"	caps	9.000 pieces
kerchiefs	85.000	"		
shoes	111.000	pairs.	total:	211 cars

- 2 -

(Page 2 of original)

3. Command of Hitler Youth Rural Service

men's old clothing	4.000	sets
men's overcoats	4.000	
men's shoes	3.000	pairs
women's old clothing	4.000	sets
women's overcoats	4.000	
women's underwear	3.000	sets
women's pullovers	20.000	
women's aprons	5.000	
scarves ,various sorts	6.000	
women's shoes	3.000	pairs

4. The enterprise "HEINRICH"

men's old clothing	2.700	sets

5. I.G.FARBENINDUSTRIE Auschwitz

men's old clothing	4.000	sets

6. Organization "TODT" - Riga

men's old clothing	1.500	sets

7. The Fuehrer's General Inspector for Motor Transport

199

men's old clothing	1.000	sets
men's underwear	1.000	"
men's shoes	1.000	"
men's overcoats	1.000	

8. Concentration camps

men's jackets	28.000	
men's pants	25.000	
men's vests	7.000	
men's shirts	44.000	
men's drawers	34.000	
men's pullovers	1.000	
men's overcoats	6.000	
women's overcoats	25.000	
men's shoes	100.000	pairs

total   44 cars
----

grand total   825 cars
=====================================

Certified true copy:

KERSTEN
SS-Hauptsturmfuehrer.

- 3 -

(Page 2 of original, cont'd)

I request SS-Obergruppenfuehrer POHL to clear up and arrange these matters to the last detail, as the strictest accuracy now will spare us much vexation later.

Heil Hitler !

yours

signed: H. HIMMLER

SS-Obergruppenfuehrer WOLFF for information.

certified: signature.

200

CERTIFICATE OF TRANSLATION

26 March 1947

I, John FOSBERRY, Civ., 20179, hereby certify that I am thoroughly conversant with the English and German languages and that the above is a true and correct translation of the original document No.NO-1257.

John FOSBERRY,
Civ., 20 179.

STAFF EVIDENCE ANALYSIS   By: Guy Favarger
                                         Date: 20 December 1946

Doc. No.   NO-1040

Title and/or general nature: Letter from Dr. Hohberg,
                                         Chief of Staff ,
                                         addressed to SS Hstf.
                                         Mellmer, dealing with a
                                         L 30.000.000.- credit
                                         from the Reinhardt Fund.

Date: 3 June 1943

Source (Location of original, etc)   OCC, WVHA Folder 7

PERSONS, FIRM OR ORGANIZATIONS   Dr. Hohberg,
           INVOLVED: SSHstuf Mellmer,
                                         SS Ogruf. Oswald Pohl,
                                         SS Gruf. Frank,
                                         SS Ostuf. Dr. Wenner,
                                         SS Standf. Joseph Vogt

TO BE FILED UNDER THESE REFERENCE   Same as above,   *Doc. 15*
              HEADINGS: NO- VHA .. A II
                                         NO-Atrocities against   **201**
                                             Civilians
                                         NO-Concentration Camps
                                         NO-Deportation
                                         NO-Jews Persecution
                                         NO-Spoliation of Foreign
                                             Property, Direct Seizure

SUMMARY (Indicate page nos).

    1. This document is a one page letter, dated 3 June 1943,
from Dr. Hohberg, Chief of Staff .., addressed to the Chief of
Office A 11, to be forwarded to SS Hstf Mellmer. It is marked
"confidential".

    2. It concerns a credit from the Reinhardt-Fund to the
Deutschen Wirtschaftsbetriebe GmbH, amounting to 30 million
marks. The interest rate will be 3%. A loan agreement shall
be drawn up between the Reich on one side and the Deutscher
Wirtschaftsbetriebe on the other. A repayment of this sum
has not been contemplated yet.

    3. SS Gruf Frank has ordered that this credit shall not
be paid out fully right away, but shall be made available in
installments.

    4. The doc. is initialed by Hohberg.

Analyst's note: Attention is drawn to Doc. 10 PS-4024, and
                        NO-554

Stab W - WL/Kü. -   Berlin, den 3.Juni 1943

An den
Chef des Amtes A II/
zur Weiterleitung an ᛋᛋ-Hauptsturmführer M e l l m e r
im H a u s e

Vertraulich!

Betr: Kredit aus dem Reinhardt-Fonds an DWB.

Nach Rücksprache mit ᛋᛋ-Obergruppenführer P o h l hat
ᛋᛋ-Gruppenführer F r a n k einen Kredit aus dem Reinhardt-
Fonds an die Deutsche Wirtschaftsbetriebe G.m.b.H. in Höhe
von RM 30.000.000,-- genehmigt. Der vereinbarungsgemäß zu
zahlende Zinssatz beträgt 3 %. Ein schriftlicher Darlehns-
vertrag soll zwischen dem Reich einerseits und den Deutschen Wirtschaftsbetrieben andererseits geschlossen werden. Es wird um Vorlegung des Vertrages gebeten. Über die
Rückzahlungstermine ist noch nichts vereinbart worden.

Gruppenführer Frank hat befohlen, daß der Kredit nicht
sofort in voller Höhe sondern abschnittweise angefordert
wird. Der Stab W (ᛋᛋ-Obersturmführer Dr. W e n n e r oder
Dr. H o h b e r g) haben mit Hauptsturmführer Mellmer
wegen der Auszahlungsmöglichkeit laufend Fühlung zu
halten.

(Dr. H o h b e r g)
Chef des Stabes W.

STAFF EVIDENCE ANALYSIS, Ministries Division.

By: Schoenfeldt.
Date: 16 December 1947.

Document Number: NG-4094.

Title and/or general nature: Notes from Dr.GOSSEL(Finance
                               Ministry) to PATZER concerning
                               the property of Jews which was
                               "found" in the Warsaw Ghetto.

Form of Document: Typescript.

Stamps and other endorsements: "Secret". Initialled by PATZER.

Date: 7 September 1944.

Source: Archivs of the former Finance
                               Ministry, Berlin-Charlottenburg
                               (OCC-BBT 6055).

PERSONS OR ORGANIZATIONS IMPLICATED: *Doc. 16*

                    GOSSEL   203
                    PATZER

TO BE FILED UNDER THESE REFERENCE HEADINGS:

                    NG-Finance Ministry.

SUMMARY:

      In his notes GOSSEL informs PATZER of an instruction
of HIMMLER with regard to the Jewish property found in the
Warsaw Ghetto. It shall be converted into money and the
proceeds be paid to the Reichs main office-counter (Reichshauptkasse) on behalf of the Minister of Finances.

      GOSSEL points to PATZER's inquiries up to now according
to which no valuables with the origin mark "Warsaw" have been
delivered to the Reichs main office-counter thus far.

          See SEA OCC-BBT 6056.

- END -

A 2070 - 12 - Gen. 17. g. BBT 6055 56 NG-4517

Ref. Dr. G o s s e l   Berlin, 7. September 1944
J 7461 - 214 I g 2.Ang.

Geheim!

Herrn
    RRechnDir P ä t z e r

      Der Reichsführer-SS und Chef der Deutschen Polizei - SS-Wirt-
schaftsverwaltungshauptamt - hat auf die Anfrage, in welcher
Weise die im Ghetto in Warschau aufgefundenen Sachwerte sicher-
gestellt und verwertet worden sind, mit Schreiben vom 25.8.1944
geantwortet, dass das im Besitz der Juden befindliche Vermögen
- soweit dies bei der Umsiedlungsaktion durch die Dienststellen der Waffen-SS beschlagnahmt wurde - verwertet und die
Erlöse an die Reichshauptkasse zugunsten des Reichsministers
der Finanzen eingezahlt worden sind.

                            Nach

204

- 2 -

Nach Jhren bisherigen Feststellungen sind bei der Reichshauptkasse Wertgegenstände mit der Herkunftsbezeichnung "Warschau" nicht
eingeliefert worden.

Jch bitte Sie um weitere Nachprüfung.

[signature]

205

STAFF EVIDENCE ANALYSIS, Ministries Division

By: Schoenfeldt
Date: 16 December 1947

Document Number: NG – 4097

Title and/or general nature: Notes by PATZER (Finance
                         Ministry) to his colleague
                         GOSSEL concerning the Jewish
                         property from the Warsaw ghetto
                         and notes by PATZER for Dr.
                         MAEDEL concerning the realiza-
                         tion of Jewish property coming
                         from concentration camps.

Form of Document: Handwritten

Doc. 17

206

Stamps and other endorsements: "Secret". Initialled by
                         PATZER, GOSSEL and MAEDEL

Date: 15 November 1944

Source: Archivs of the former Finance
                         Ministry, Berlin – Charlotten-
                         burg.
                              OCC – BET 6056

PERSONS OR ORGANIZATIONS IMPLICATED:

                         PATZER
                         GOSSEL
                         MAEDEL

TO BE FILED UNDER THESE REFERENCE HEADINGS:

                         NG – Finance Ministry

SUMMARY:
        This is PATZER's answer to GOSSEL's note of 7
September 1944. PATZER states that no valuables from the
Warsaw ghetto have been delivered to the main office –
counter nor can they be expected in the future. The reason
for this is that the proceeds are paid to the account
"Max Heiliger" and from time to time taken into the Reich
budget where they are booked in plan XVII, chapter 7,
title 3. (Analyst's note: This is the chapter of "Miscellaneous income".)

- 1 -   over

In the second part of his notes PATZER informs
MAEDEL that he is not in a position to give exact information about the realization of the Jewish property found
in concentration camps, as he did not participate in the
discussion with the "SS economic - administrative main
office" on 24. July 1944. This is the answer to a letter
from MAEDEL.

See SEA NG - 4096 and 4094.

207

-2-
END

Sachbearbeiter
Reg. Rat Puhar
A 2070 - 12 - Zu b. g.
g. schrb. 11

Berlin, 16. November 1944

Geheim!

An Herrn Reg.-Rat Grosse
Abt. I

Verwertung von Judenvermögen
Ihr Schreiben vom 7. September 1944 D VI 6 - 214 I g 2.Ang.

Ich habe bei der Reichshauptkasse neuerdings festgestellt, daß bei ihr Wertgegenstände mit der Herkunftsbezeichnung "Überführt" nicht eingeliefert worden sind.
Es ist noch einem mir ungesichten bekannt gewordenen
Schreiben des Chefs des SS-Wirtschafts-Verwaltungshauptamts vom 24. Juli 1944 A II/3 Reinh./Ma./Kr. Geh.
Tgb.Nr. 66/44 nicht mit dem Zugang solcher Wertgegenstände bei der Reichshauptkasse mehr zu rechnen, weil
deren Verwertung in der folgenden Weise vor sich
geht:

Fkf. setzt in die Reichsbank ein mit der Anlage
des Schreibens des Reg. Mödel vom 18.8.44
vorgesehen den Teil.

Die auf dem Konto "Max Heiliger" bei der Reichshauptkasse stehenden Gelder werden von Zeit zu Zeit
durch das Reg. Mödel der Abt. VIII (früher Abt. IX)
haushaltsmäßig abgewickelt. Die Erträge werden
nach dem Einzelplan XVII Kap. 7 Tit. 3 abgeführt und ein-
gebucht.

2.

2) Herrn Reg. Dr. Mödel
Abt. VIII

Heranziehung von Judenvermögen
Ihr Schreiben vom 18. August 1944 O 5400 - 32/44 VI

Ich bin leider nicht in der Lage, Ihnen über die Heranziehung des in Konzentrationslagern anfallenden Judenvermögens näher Auskunft zu geben. Ich habe an den in dem Schreiben des Chefs des SS-Wirtschafts-Verwaltungshauptamts vom 24. Juli 1944 erwähnten Besprechungen nicht teilgenommen. Die diesbezügl. Angaben in dem eben bezeichneten Schreiben beruht auf einem Irrtum. Ich halte mein Referat in dieser Angelegenheit auch nicht für hervorstechend.

Die in der Anlage zu Ihrem Schreiben vom 18. August 1944 erwähnte Abschrift der Mitteilung an den Rechnungshof des Deutschen Reichs vom 19. November 1943 ist nach Angabe der Registratur I im R Fall nicht zu ermitteln. Sie ist vermutlich bei den von im R Fall vom 23. November 1943 vernichtet worden, bevor sie in die Registratur gelangte.

Die Beantwortung Ihres Schreibens soll sich wegen der Nachforschung nach dem Vorgängen... verzögert.

im RFU
vernichtet

3) Reg. Gen. L.
der Vorgang J 3030-89 I
vom 19.10.43 ist an die Reg I zurück-
zugeben.
4) Nach Erledigung an Handakte
5) Akten

OFFICE OF CHIEF OF COUNSEL FOR WAR CRIMES
APO 696 A   U.S. ARMY

STAFF EVIDENCE ANALYSIS: By: Hans Fiskus
- - - - - - - - - - - - -   Date: 15 September 1947

Doc. No.   NO- 5193

Title and/or general nature: a) Cover letter bearing the letter-
                                head of the Inspector of Sta-
                                tistics, addressed to SS Ostubaf.
                                Dr. R. BRANDT, signed by Dr. KOR-
                                HERR.
                             b) " The Final Solution of the
                                Jewish Problem in Europe".
                                Statistical report.

Date: 19 April 1943

Doc. 18

Source(Location of original,   7771 Document Center Berlin
        etc.)   Shelf M Special I -7
                                     SS- 4075

210

PERSONS, FIRMS OR ORGAN-   Adolf HITLER
IZATIONS IMPLICATED: RFSS
                                Chief of Sipo and SD
                                P. KORHERR, Inspector of
                                     Statistics
                                SS Ostubaf. BRANDT
                                RSHA
                                SS General

TO BE FILED UNDER THESE   NO- as above
REFERENCE HEADINGS: NO- Persecution of Jews
                                NO- Atrocities against Civilians
                                NO- Genocide
                                NO- Concentration Camps
                                NO- WVHA
                                NO- RSHA
                                NO- Einsatzgruppen

SUMMARY: (indicate page No.)

a)   This is a one-page cover letter, bearing the letterhead
   of the Inspector of Statistics , addressed to SS Ostubaf.
   Dr. BRANDT, signed by KORHERR. It is classified " top secret"
   and bears the handwritten note: " to be filed " and Rudolf
   BRANDT's initials.

                        -1-   - over -

KORHERR refers to his report intended for the RFSS (see
SS- 4074) as well as to an RFSS order dated 1 April 1943, addressed to the Chief of Sipo and SD, and concerning the compil-
ing of a shortened report to be submitted to the Fuehrer. To
comply with this order KORHERR states he had transmitted the
attached report of 6½ pages to the RSHA.

Unfortunately, KORHERR states, due to difficulties arising
from the nature of the subject, it is impossible to show exact
figures on Jews assigned to work, Jews held in Concentration
Camps and in Ghettos for aged Jews, and Jews living in mixed
marriage privileged by German law, so that all the other Jews
could be evacuated. Also figures on Jews in Concentration Camps
and on Jewish labor are not exact as far as their location and
nationality are concerned.

b)   This is a seven pages report on the Final Solution of the
Jewish Problem in Europe, classified " top secret", originating from Pg. Dr. KORHERR, Inspector of Statistics.

211

This report is a digest from the 16 page report on the same
subject (see SS 4074). It contains, however, the following
additional figures.

During the period from 1 January 1943 to 31 March 1943 again
113,015 Jews were "evacuated" from the Reich, the Protectorate
and the Incorporated Eastern Territories, and 8,025 Jews taken
to the Concentration Camp for aged Jews in Theresienstadt(p.5)

On 1 April 1943 only 31,910 Jews were left in the old parts
of the Reich.(p.5)
16, 668 of them are living in mixed marriage. 12,117 of these
mixed marriages are privileged.(p.5)
During the first three months of the year 1943 further 49,254
Jews were " evacuated" from France, Netherlands, Belgium, Norway,
Slovakia and Kroatia(see report SS 4074), and for the first
time also from Greece and Bulgaria.

See also SS 4070, 4071, 4072. 4073, 4074.

-2-
-End -

Der Inspekteur für Statistik (qu 1572/43) Berlin W 35, 19.4.1943
Tgb.Nr. 48/43 geh.Rs. Potsdamer Straße 61

Geheime Reichssache

SS-Obersturmbannführer Dr.R. B r a n d t
Pers.Stab Reichsführer-SS
B e r l i n

Lieber Pg. B r a n d t !

Mein kürzlicher Bericht über die Endlösung der Judenfrage
mit 16 Seiten Umfang war von mir zur Berichtung an den RF
erstellt worden, wie mir der RF mündlich befohlen hatte.

Gemäß dem neuen Befehl des Reichsführers vom 1.4.1943 an
den Chef der Sicherheitspolizei und des SD zur Erstellung
eines gekürzten Berichtes zur Vorlage an den Führer mit
eindeutiger Bilanz habe ich vor einigen Tagen dem Reichssicherheitshauptamt den in Abschrift beifolgenden Bericht
von 6 1/2 Seiten zur Einarbeitung in seinen Gesamtbericht
zugeleitet.

Ich darf dazu, falls der RF nicht ganz einverstanden sein
sollte, bemerken: Eine eindeutige Bilanz für einen festen
Zeitraum für das ganze heutige Reich läßt sich trotz alles
vergossenen Schweißes nicht erstellen. Ich habe darum neben
einer Gesamtbilanz mit wechselndem Anfangszeitpunkt verschiedene Teilbilanzen gebracht. Die vorhandenen verschie-
denen Anfangs- und Schlußzahlen differieren z.T. um hundert-
tausende von Juden. Die vorhandenen Juden lassen sich
auch mit den vorhandenen Unterlagen nicht, wie es wün-
schenswert wäre, nach Juden im Arbeitseinsatz, in KL's,
im Altersghetto, in privilegierter Mischehe teilen, sodaß
der verbleibende Rest sofort für die Evakuierung zur Ver-
fügung steht. Sowohl beim Arbeitseinsatz wie in den KL's
lassen die bisherigen Unterlagen keine zuverlässigen
Schlüsse bezüglich der räumlichen Zugehörigkeit der Juden
(von der Staatsangehörigkeit abgesehen) zu. Darum mußte
ich hier eine eindeutige Bilanz vermeiden, doch geben
die Zahlen an sich einen brauchbaren Anhaltspunkt.

1 Anlage g.Rs.   H e i l H i t l e r !

212

NO - 5193

DIE ENDLÖSUNG DER EUROPÄISCHEN JUDENFRAGE
==
Statistischer Bericht

__Notwendige Vorbemerkung__. Judenstatistiken sind immer mit
Vorbehalt aufzunehmen, da bei der zahlenmäßigen Erfassung
des Judentums stets mit besonderen Fehlern zu rechnen ist.
Fehlerquellen liegen u.a. in Wesen und Entwicklung des
Judentums, seiner Abgrenzung, seiner mehrtausendjährigen
ruhelosen Wanderschaft, den zahllosen Aufnahmen und Austritten, den Angleichungsbestrebungen, der Vermischung mit
den Wirtsvölkern, vor allem aber im Bemühen des Juden, sich
der Erfassung zu entziehen.

Schließlich hat die Statistik teils als Notbehelf, teils
wegen der weitgehenden Übereinstimmung zwischen jüdischer
Rasse und jüdischem Glauben, teils im konfessionellen
Denken des letzten Jahrhunderts befangen, bis zuletzt die
Juden nicht nach ihrer Rasse, sondern nach ihrem religiösen
Bekenntnis erfaßt. Die Erfassung der Juden nach der Rasse
gestaltet sich auch -vor allem durch die äußerliche Ver-
kleinerung des Judentums infolge Austritt, Übertritt,
weiter zurückliegender rassischer Vermischung und durch
Tarnung- sehr schwierig, wie die mißlungene Erfassung der
Rassejuden in Österreich 1923 und die Erhebung der Voll-,
Halb- und Vierteljuden bei der deutschen Volkszählung 1939
zeigen. Jüdische Bestandszahlen sind im allgemeinen nur als
Mindestzahlen zu werten, wobei der Fehler mit geringerem
jüdischem Blutanteil immer größer wird.

Fast unüberwindliche Schwierigkeiten bereitet die Erstellung
einer einigermaßen zuverlässigen Statistik über Bestand und
Bewegung des Judentums in den gesamten Ostgebieten seit
Beginn des zweiten Weltkrieges, der unkontrollierbare
Massen von Juden in Bewegung gebracht hat.

NO- 5193

BILANZ DES JUDENTUMS

W e l t . Die Gesamtzahl der Juden auf der Erde schätzte man im letzten Jahrzehnt auf 15 bis 18 Millionen, zuweilen auch auf weit über 20 Millionen. Das Statistische Reichsamt gab für das Jahr 1937 die Zahl mit <u>17 Millionen</u> an.

E u r o p a . Davon leben um 1937 etwa <u>10,3 Millionen(60vH)</u> <u>in Europa</u> und 5,1 Millionen(30 vH) in Amerika. Um 1880 hatte der europäische Anteil noch 88 vH, der amerikanische erst gut 3 vH betragen.

In Europa häufen bzw. häuften sich die Juden vor allem in den nunmehr von Deutschland besetzten früheren polnisch-russischen und baltischen Gebieten zwischen Ostsee und Finnischem Meerbusen und dem Schwarzen und Asowschen Meer, daneben in den Handelsmittelpunkten Mittel- und Westeuropas, im Rheingebiet und an den Küsten des Mittelmeers.

D e u t s c h l a n d . Die Judenbilanz des Reiches ist an die verschieden großen Zeiträume seit der jeweiligen Machtübernahme in seinen Teilgebieten gebunden. Erst von diesen Zeitpunkten an beginnt das Abfluten der Juden in großem Stil. Vorher gab es in manchen Gebieten sogar eine Zunahme der Juden als Folge des Abflusses aus Gebieten, die zum Reiche kamen.

214

Zur Zeit der jeweiligen Machtübernahme und am 31.12.1942 betrug die Zahl der Juden in

Gebiet	Zeitpunkt der Machtübernahme	Zahl der Juden vor der Machtübernahme	am 31.12.1942
Altreich	30.1.1933	561 000 }	51 327
Sudetenland	29.9.1938	30 000 }	
Ostmark	13.3.1938	220 000	8 102
Böhmen und Mähren	16.3.1939	118 000	15 550
Ostgebiete (mit Bialystok)	Sept.1939 (Juni 1940)	790 000	233 210
Generalgouv. (mit Lemberg)	Sept.1939 (Juni 1940)	2 000 000	297 914
<u>Z u s a m m e n</u>	-	<u>3 719 000</u>	<u>606 103</u>

NC - 5193

Zu den Zahlen vor der jeweiligen Machtübernahme ist ergänzend zu bemerken, daß sie z.T. ineinanderfließen. So strömte der Großteil der 30 000 Juden des Sudetenlandes (27 000 Glaubensjuden) vor der Vereinigung mit dem Reich ohne Überschreitung einer Staatsgrenze und ohne Vermögensverluste rasch ins Protektorat ab, ist also in den Zahlen für Böhmen und Mähren von 1939 zu einem Teil wieder enthalten. Das Sudetenland zählte am 17.5.1939 nur mehr 2 649 Juden.

Für die Zeit kurz vor dem zweiten Weltkrieg läßt sich die Zahl der Juden im Reichsgebiet mit Protektorat und Generalgouvernement für einen festen Zeitpunkt angeben bzw. abschätzen. Sie beträgt um den 17.5.1939 in

			Zum Vergleich: am 31.12.1942
Altreich		233 973	} 51 327
Sudetenland		2 649	
Ostmark		94 270	8 102
Böhmen und Mähren		110 000	15 550
Ostgebiete	rd.	790 000	233 210
Generalgouv.	rd.	2 000 000	297 914
Zusammen		3 120 892	606 103

215

Altreich und Ostmark hatten bis zum Kriege weit über die Hälfte ihres -zivilisierten und sterilen- Judenbestandes bereits abgegeben, vor allem durch Auswanderung, während im Osten der Zusammenbruch der für die Zukunft gefährlichen fruchtbaren Judenmassen überwiegend erst im Kriege und besonders seit den Evakuierungsmaßnahmen von 1942 deutlich wird.

Das Judentum hat sich damit von 1933 bis 1943 innerhalb des erweiterten Reichsgebietes, also im zeitlich-räumlichen Bereich der nationalsozialistischen Staatsführung, um rund 3 , 1 Millionen Köpfe vermindert. Im Altreich sank der Bestand auf fast 1/12, in der Ostmark gar auf 1/27, im Generalgouvernement und in Böhmen und Mähren auf etwa 1/7, in den Ostgebieten auf 1/3 bis 1/4.

NO-5193

Auswanderung, Sterbeüberschuß und Evakuierung. Dieser Rückgang ist das Ergebnis des Zusammenwirkens von Auswanderung, Sterbeüberschuß und Evakuierung, wozu noch geringfügige sonstige Veränderungen kommen (z.B. genehmigte Austritte, Anerkennung als Mischling I.Grades, Neuerfassung, Karteibereinigung), worüber die folgende Tabelle Aufschluß gibt:

Gebiet	Zeitraum von .... bis 31.12.1942	Abnahme (-) oder Zunahme der Juden durch				
		Auswanderung	Sterbe-überschuß	Evakuierung	Sonst. Veränderg.	Insgesamt
Altreich (mit Sudetenland	30.1.33 (29.9.38)	-382 534	-61 193	- 100 516	+4 570	- 539 673
Ostmark	13.3.38	-149 124	-14 509	- 47 555	- 710	- 211 898
Böhmen und Mähren	16.3.39	- 25 699	- 7 074	- 69 677	-	- 102 450
Ostgebiete (mit Bialystok)	Sept.39 (Juni 40)	- 334 673		- 222 117	-	- 556 790
Generalgouv. (mit Lemberg)	Sept.39 (Juni 40)	- 427 920		-1 274 166	-	-1 702 086
Zusammen		-1 402 726		-1 714 031	+3 860	-3 112 897

216

Die Bilanz für Altreich, Ostmark und Böhmen und Mähren zusammen sieht folgendermaßen aus:

```
Anfangsbestand der Juden
   bei jeweil.Machtübernahme:      929 000
   Veränderungen durch:
      Auswanderung               - 557 357
      Sterbeüberschuß            -  82 776
      Evakuierung                - 217 748
      Neuerfassung usw.          +   3 860
                                 - 854 021
Bestand am 31.12.1942:            74 979
```

Der außerordentliche Sterbeüberschuß der Juden z.B. im Altreich ist infolge der anormalen Überalterung und Lebensschwäche des Judentums ebenso auf Geburtenarmut wie auf hohe Sterblichkeit zurückzuführen: im 1.Viertel 1943 zählte man 22 Geburten, 1 113 Sterbefälle. Die Zahlen über Auswanderung und Sterbeüberschuß(Kriegswirren!) der Ostgebiete und des Generalgouvernements sind nicht nachprüfbar. Sie sind das berechnete

NO-5193

Ergebnis aus Anfangs- und Endbestand und Evakuierungen der Juden.

Vom 1.1.1943 bis 31.3.1943 fand aus dem Reichsgebiet mit Böhmen und Mähren, neuen Ostgebieten und Bezirk Bialystok wieder die Evakuierung von 113 015 Juden nach dem Osten statt, ebenso die Wohnsitzverlegung von 8 025 Juden ins Altersghetto Theresienstadt. Die Judenzahl in Deutschland, namentlich in den Ostgebieten, wurde dadurch neuerdings stark herabgesetzt.

<u>Mischehen.</u> Die Zahl der Juden im Reichsgebiet von 1939 enthält am 31.12.1942 einen nicht geringen Teil von Juden in Mischehen:

	Juden am 31.12.42	davon in Mischehe	Rest
Altreich	51 327	16 760	34 567
Ostmark	8 102	4 803	3 299
Böhmen und Mähren	15 550	6 211	9 339
<u>Zusammen</u>	<u>74 979</u>	<u>27 774</u>	<u>47 205</u>

217

Die Judenzahl des Altreichs hat sich inzwischen weiter von 51 327 am 31.12.1942 auf <u>31 910 am 1.4.1943</u> vermindert. Unter diesen 31 910 Juden leben über die Hälfte, nämlich 16 668 in Mischehe, davon 12 117 in privilegierter und 4 551 in nicht privilegierter Mischehe. Außerdem dürfte in der Aufstellung noch eine größere Anzahl von Juden mitgezählt sein, die schließlich als unauffindbar abgeschrieben werden müssen, wie es auch bei jedem Einwohnerkataster immer wieder vorkommt. Der Bestand der Juden im alten Reichsgebiet(ohne Ostgebiete) nähert sich seinem Ende.

<u>Arbeitseinsatz.</u> Von den im Reichsgebiet lebenden Juden befanden sich zu Beginn des Jahres 1943

   21 659 in kriegswichtigem Arbeitseinsatz.

Dazu kommen in kriegswichtigem Arbeitseinsatz 18 435 sowjetrussische Juden im Inspekteur-Bereich Königsberg, 50 570 staatenlose und ausländische Juden im Lagereinsatz Schmelt (Breslau) und 95 112 ehem.polnische Juden im Ghetto- und Lagereinsatz im Inspekteur-Bereich Posen.

NO-5193

Konzentrationslager. In Konzentrationslagern befanden sich am 31.12.1942 insgesamt 9 127 Juden, in Justizvollzugsanstalten 458 Juden. Die Belegstärke der Konzentrationslager mit Juden war folgende:

		Mauthausen/Gusen	79
Lublin	7 342	Sachsenhausen	46
Auschwitz	1 412	Stutthof	18
Buchenwald	227	Ravensbrück	3.

Altersghetto. Im einzigen Altersghetto Theresienstadt gab es Anfang 1943 zusammen 49 392 Juden, die von den Bestandszahlen abgeschrieben sind.

Evakuierung aus anderen europäischen Ländern. Im deutschen Macht- und Einflußbereich außerhalb der Reichsgrenzen fanden folgende Evakuierungen von Juden statt:

218

Länder	bis 31.12.42	im 1.Vierteljahr 1943
Frankreich (soweit vor dem 10.11.42 besetzt)	41 911	7 995
Niederlande	38 571	13 832
Belgien	16 886	1 616
Norwegen	532	158
Griechenland	-	13 435
Slowakei	56 691	854
Kroatien	4 927	-
Bulgarien	-	11 364
Außerdem in den russischen Gebieten einschl. der früheren baltischen Länder seit Beginn des Ostfeldzuges	633 300	-
Zusammen	792 818	49 254

Europäische Judenbilanz. Die Verminderung des Judentums in Europa dürfte damit bereits an 4 Millionen Köpfe betragen. Höhere Judenbestände zählen auf dem europ. Kontinent (neben Rußland mit etwa 4 Mill.) nur noc Ungarn (750 000) und Rumänien (302 000), vielleicht noch Frankreich. Berücksichtigt man neben dem angeführten Rückgang die jüdische Auswanderung und den jüdischen Sterbeüberschuf

in den außerdeutschen Staaten Mittel- und Westeuropas, aber
auch die unbedingt vorkommenden Doppelzählungen infolge der
jüdischen Fluktuation, dann dürfte die Verminderung des Judentums in Europa von 1937 bis Anfang 1943 auf 4 1/2 Millionen zu schätzen sein. Dabei konnte von den Todesfällen der
sowjet-russischen Juden in den besetzten Ostgebieten nur ein
Teil erfaßt werden, während diejenigen im übrigen europäischen Rußland und an der Front überhaupt nicht enthalten
sind. Dazu kommen die Wanderungsströme der Juden innerhalb
Rußlands in den asiatischen Bereich hinüber. Auch der Wanderungsstrom der Juden aus den europäischen Ländern außerhalb des deutschen Einflußbereichs nach Übersee ist eine
weitgehend unbekannte Größe.

Insgesamt dürfte das europäische Judentum seit 1933, also
im ersten Jahrzehnt der nationalsozialistischen Machtentfaltung, bald die Hälfte seines Bestandes verloren haben.
Davon ist wieder nur etwa die Hälfte, also ein Viertel des
europäischen Gesamtbestandes von 1937, den anderen Erdtei-
len zugeflossen.

219

OFFICE OF CHIEF OF COUNSEL FOR WAR CRIMES
APO 696A   U.S. ARMY

STAFF EVIDENCE ANALYSIS   By; Hans Fiskus
                                 Date: 15 September 1947

Doc. No.:   NO-5194

Title and/or general nature: "The final Solution of the
                                 Jewish Problem in Europe".
                                 Statistical Report issued by
                                 the Inspector for Statistics
                                 with the RF-SS.

Date: March 1943.

Source (Location of original, etc.): 7771 Document Center Berlin
                                 Shelf M Special I-7
                                 SS - 4074

PERSONS, FIRMS OR ORGANIZATIONS
            IMPLICATED: RFSS
                                Dr. KORHERR, Inspector for
                                     Statistics
                                RSHA (Main Reich Security Office
                                Chief of SIPO and SD
                                SS General

TO BE FILED UNDER THESE REFERENCE
            HEADINGS: As above
                                NO-Atrocities against
                                     Civilians
                                NO-Persecution of Jews
                                NO-Genocide
                                NO-Concentration camps
                                NO-WVHA
                                NO-RSHA
                                NO-Einsatzgruppen

Doc. 19

220

SUMMARY (Indicate page nos.)

      This is a 16 page statistical report, marked "Top
Secret", on the "Final Solution of the Jewish Problem in
Europe" originating from Dr. KORHERR, Inspector for
Statistics on the Staff of RF-SS. The document bears
Himmler's initials and the date 27 March 1943 apparently
written by Himmler, thus indicating that it has been read
by him.

      (Analyst's note: It appears from documents SS-4071
and SS-4073 that the original text of page 9 had been changed
on Himmler's order. Apparently the whole page 9 has been
exchanged by Korherr before the report was returned to
Himmler).

(I) In the introductory remarks, (Analyst's note: the author
of the Report) emphasizes the difficulties arising from the
nature of the subject (p.1-3).

(II)In the following section of the report, Korherr indicates
that the total number of Jews in the old parts of the Reich
(Germany proper) during the period from 30 January 1933 to
1   ed from   561,040 (without Sudetengau
                                          and Danzig)
                                  51,327 (including Sudetengau
                                          and Danzig)
A   -vacuated".

                              ecreased during the period

1 March 1938 to 1 January 1943
                from   220,000
                to   8,102₁
47,555 Jews were "evacuated" during this period.

3) In the Protectorate (Bohemia and Moravia) the number
of Jews decreased during the period from 15 March 1939 to
1 January 1943
                from   · 102,760
                to   15,550.
69,677 Jews were "evacuated" during this time.

The decrease of the number of Jews living in all these
areas was due to "evacuations", emigrations, to the fact
that the death-rate exceeded by far the number of births,
and, to a small extent, to various reasons.

4) The number of Jews living in the Eastern Territories
(without Danzig) incorporated into the Reich at the
moment of the occupation can only be estimated and amounted
to about 2,5 Million at the end of 1939.

Korherr points out that in the old parts of the Reich
including the Sudetengau the number of Jews amounted to
only 9,2 % (74,979) of the total existing on the day of
the Machtuebernahme (accession to Power) and had further
decreased to 7,9 % (44,589) on 28 February 1943 (p.3-5).

(III) Korherr emphasizes the fact that the rather high
death-rate of the German Jews exceeded by far the
extremely low number of births.   Due to a certain lack
of information especially with regard to the death-rate in the
concentration camps, only an estimate can be made.   Even so,
the deat-rate of Jews in Germany proper and the Sudetengau
amounted to 80 to 85 whilst the European average (1942)
was 10 to 15 per mille.   The birth-rate is extremely low
(7 Jewish children in January 1943, 8 Jewish children in
February 1943 were born within the Reich), the number of
suicides far above the average (p.5-8).

(IV) The following part of the Report deals with the
emigration stressing the fact that due to the lack of exact
information the figures indicated in the Report are based
on estimates giving figures between 200,000 and 530,000
(p.7-8).

(V) The "Evacuation" (Analyst's note: Actually deportation)
of Jews succeeded the period of Emigration when Jews were
forbidden in the fall of 1941 to emigrate from the Reich.
The terms officially used for this deportation are
"Abwanderung" (Migration) and "Evakuierung" (Evacuation).

According to the statistics of the RSHA "migrated" until
1 January 1943 from the old parts of the Reich (including
the Sudetengau)
                                 100,516 Jews
        from Austria   47,555   "
        from the Protectorate _ _ 69,677 _ _ "_ _ _
                                 217,748 Jews.

During the period from October 1939 to 31 December 1942 a
total of 1,873,549 Jews were "evacuated" from the Reich,
the occupied Eastern Territories and other European
countries under German control (viz. France, Netherlands,
Belgium, Norway, Slovakia, Kroatia).   This figure includes
people subjected to "special treatment" (Analyst's note:
that means: killed) and 87,193 persons sent to the
concentration camp for aged Jews in Theresienstadt.

- 2 -

221

Furthermore, according to information given by the RSHA 633,300 Jews were evacuated from Russian areas and the former Baltic States.

Korherr points out that the number of inmates of Concentration Camps and Ghettos are not included in the above figures, and that the "evacuation" of Jews from Slovakia and Kroatia has been carried out by these States (p.9-10).

(VI) The Report shows the following figures on Jews held in Ghettos._ A total of 87,193 Jews had been sent from the Reich and the Protectorate to the Ghetto for aged Jews in Theresienstadt. This number decreased mainly by the death of inmates to 49,392 at the beginning of the year 1943.

The Litzmannstadt Ghetto had at the same time 87,180 inmates.

The Jewish population of the Government General, mainly held in Ghettos ("Restghettos") amounted to 297,914. (p.10-11).

(VII) Jews_in Concentration Camps.
During the period from the day of the accession to Power till 31 December 1942

  73,417 Jews were sent to concentration camps
  36,943 Jews were released
  27,347 died
  9,127 Jews were still held in concentration camps on 31 December 1942.

This figure does not include the number of Jews taken to the concentration camps Auschwitz (Oswiecim) and Lublin within the scope of the "evacuation" program.

On page 12 the report breaks down figures concerning the various concentration camps, indicating for instance that out of 23,409 men sent to the Lublin C.C. 4,509 were released
  and 14,217 died
" " 2,849 women " " " " C.C. 59 were released
  and 131 died
" " 4,917 men " " " Auschwitz CC 1 was released
  and 3,716 died
" " 932 women " " " " C.C. nobody was released
  and 720 died
" " 231 men in Gross-Rosen C.C. nobody was released,
  all 231 died
" " 192 men in Neuengamme C.C. 2 were released
  and 190 died
" " 80 men in Flossenbuerg C.C. 2 were released
  and 78 died
" " 12,026 men sent to Dachau C.C. 886 died
" " 16,827 " " " Buchenwald CC. 2,795 died
" " 2,064 " " " Mauthausen CC 1,985 died

It can be assumed that figures appearing under the heading "released from CC.'s" include those persons who were not set free but transferred from one C.C. to another.

(VIII) At the beginning of 1943 a total of 458 Jews were held in various prisons located in the Reich. (p.12).

(IX) At the beginning of the year 1943, 185,776 Jews had been assigned to war work within the Reich including Jews of foreign (especially Russian and Polish) nationality and 50,670 stateless and foreign Jews working with the Organization Schmelt in Breslau. (p.12-13).

(X) The last part of the report gives an overall view on the developments in the Jewish populations.

Korherr estimates that during 1937 to 1942 the Jewish population of Europe has decreased by about 4 million persons not including Russian Jews who "died" in the occupied Eastern Territories, were lost in action or migrated to other regions in Russia.

Concluding his report he stresses the fact that the Jewish population of Europe has been halved during the first ten years of the Nazi Regime.

See also SS 4070, 4071, 4072, 4073, 4075, 4076.

223

Geheime Reichssache

NO - 5194

2/ III 1...

DIE ENDLÖSUNG DER EUROPÄISCHEN JUDENFRAGE

Statistischer Bericht

I n h a l t :

———

DIE ENDLÖSUNG DER EUROPÄISCHEN JUDENFRAGE
Statistischer Bericht

I. VORBEMERKUNG

Zur Aufstellung einer Bilanz über die Ergebnisse auf dem
Wege zur Lösung der Judenfrage bedarf es der zahlenmäßigen
Erfassung des Judentums und seiner Entwicklung. Die Wider-
sprüche in den Zahlenangaben über das Judentum machen jedoch eine Vorbemerkung dahingehend nötig, daß Zahlen über
das Judentum stets mit besonderem Vorbehalt aufzunehmen
sind und ohne Kenntnis ihrer Quelle und Entstehung oft zu
Fehlschlüssen führen. Die Fehlerquellen liegen vor allem
im Wesen des Judentums und seiner historischen Entwicklung,
in seiner tausendjährigen ruhelosen Wanderschaft, den zahllosen Aufnahmen und Austritten, den Angleichungsbestrebungen, der Vermischung mit den Wirtsvölkern, in dem Bemühen
des Juden, sich unbemerkt der Erfassung zu entziehen, und
schließlich in falschen oder falsch ausgelegten Statistiken
über das Judentum.

225

Darüber hinaus hat die Statistik -teils als statistischen
Notbehelf, teils wegen der weitgehenden Übereinstimmung
zwischen jüdischem Glauben und jüdischer Rasse, teils in
Unkenntnis des Rassegedankens, teils im religiösen Denken
der jeweiligen Zeit befangen- bis zuletzt die Juden fast
nie nach ihrer Rasse, sondern nach ihrem religiösen Bekenntnis erfaßt. Die Erfassung der Rasse setzt eine vieljährige
Schulung und auch Ahnenforschung voraus. Auch gestaltete
sie sich schwierig, vor allem in südlichen und östlichen
Ländern, weil trotz aller Übereinstimmung eine einheitliche
jüdische Rasse sich statistisch schwer abgrenzen ließ. Das
Bekenntnis zum mosaischen oder israelitischen Glauben ist
wieder kein vollgültiges Beweismittel, weil es infolge der
einstigen jüdischen Missionsbewegung mit ihrer Aufnahme von
Massen von Heiden und Christen, auch durch die Übertritte
zum Judentum in neuer Zeit durch Mischehen und "Bekehrung"
nicht wenige Glaubensjuden nichtjüdischer Rasse gibt, wäh-

rend

rend umgekehrt das Zwangschristentum und die im letzten
Jahrhundert wieder stark angestiegene Zahl der getauften
Juden und daneben der Gemeinschaftslosen mit jüdischer
Rasse die Judenzahl drückten. So schätzte Leroy-Beaulieu
1893 den Verlust des Judentums durch das Christentum auf
das Vier- bis Zehnfache seiner heutigen Anhänger, nach
Maurice Fishberg und Mathias Mieses ist das Dreifache der
heutigen Judenzahl im arischen Europa aufgegangen. Sogar
Hans Günther schätzt die Zahl der Juden in Deutschland auf
das Doppelte der Zahl der Juden mosaischen Glaubens, die
deutsche Staatsangehörige sind. Schließlich geht der litau-
ische Jude Brutzkus so weit, die Berliner Juden nach ihrer
Blutzusammensetzung als reinere Europäer zu bezeichnen als
die Deutschen in Berlin.

Entsprechend diesen Meinungen hat man die Anteile der Rassejuden samt Mischlingen in Europa vielfach dreimal so hoch
als die der Glaubensjuden angenommen (in Osteuropa zweimal,
in Mitteleuropa viermal, im übrigen Europa gar achtmal so
hoch) und mit etwa 6 vH mehr oder weniger jüdischem Blut in
der europäischen Bevölkerung gerechnet. Demgegenüber führte
Burgdörfer die Judenzahlen für das Deutschland von 1933 auf
850 000 Voll-, Halb- und Vierteljuden (bei 502 799 Glaubensjuden) in seinen Schätzungen zurück, für Österreich von 1934
auf 300-400 000 (bei 191 481 Glaubensjuden). Die Erhebung
der Rassejuden bei der deutschen Volkszählung von 1939 hat
bei 307 614 Glaubensjuden nur die etwas höhere Zahl von
330 892 Volljuden, 72 738 Halbjuden und 42 811 Vierteljuden
ergeben, die vor allem bezüglich der Halb- und Vierteljuden
keinesfalls als zuverlässig angesehen werden kann. Die ge-
wonnenen Zahlen lassen sich nur als Mindestzahlen werten.
Sie kamen durch die in einer "Ergänzungskarte" zur Haus-
haltungsliste der Volkszählung 1939 enthaltene Frage "War
oder ist einer der 4 Großelternteile Volljude?" zustande,
die für jeden Großelternteil mit "ja" oder mit "nein" zu
beantworten war. Da diese Ergänzungskarte in verschlosse-
nem Umschlag abzugeben und darum der Kontrolle am Ort ent-
zogen war, wurde sie schlecht ausgefüllt. Vielfach wurden

statt

NC - 5194

statt einer Antwort nur Striche in die entsprechenden Fächer gemacht.

Der erste amtliche Versuch, die Juden nach ihrer Rasse zu erfassen, wurde von den Juden sofort sabotiert. Er geschah bei der österreichischen Volkszählung vom 7. März 1923. Vizekanzler Dr. Frank (Großdeutsche Volkspartei) unterzeichnete kurz vor der Zählung eine Verordnung, wonach zur Frage 7 des Zählblattes (Sprache) "auch die Volkszugehörigkeit und Rasse anzugeben" waren. Da die Zählblätter bereits gedruckt waren, wurde darauf nur in einem roten Merkzettel ohne Erläuterung, Anleitung und Musterbeispiele hingewiesen. Die österreichischen Juden sabotierten diese Frage dadurch, daß die jüdisch-marxistische Presse unmittelbar vor dem Zählungstag ihre Leser aufforderte, die Frage nach der Rasse mit " w e i ß " zu beantworten. Das Ergebnis war, daß daraufhin die "weiße Rasse in Österreich etwa so weit verbreitet war, wie die Einflußsphäre der jüdisch-marxistischen Presse und Parteien reichte". Nur in Kärnten und im Burgenland wurde die Aufbereitung des Materials mit recht zweifelhaftem Erfolg durchgeführt, in den anderen Bundesländern und vor allem in Wien aber als zwecklos eingestellt.

227

II. DIE JUDENBILANZ IN DEUTSCHLAND

Die folgenden Angaben über die Zahl und Entwicklung der Juden in Deutschland fußen auf den amtlichen Zahlen der Volkszählungen und sonstigen Erhebungen des Reiches und auf den Berechnungen und Schätzungen der Wissenschaft, sind aber in der Hauptsache von der Reichsvereinigung der Juden in Deutschland und von den Kultusgemeinden in Wien und Prag erstellt, die mit Zählungen, Zählkarten für die Bevölkerungsbewegung, Fortschreibung und daneben mit Berechnungen und Schätzungen arbeiten. Diese jüdischen Dienststellen arbeiten unter der Kontrolle des Reichssicherheitshauptamtes und für dessen Zwecke. Vom fraglichen Anfangsbestand der Juden abgesehen scheint die Reichsvereinigung der Juden in Deutschland zuverlässig zu arbeiten. Aufgrund der an dieser Stelle gefertigten und vom Reichssicherheitshauptamt bislang überprüften Statistiken kann folgende Bilanz über die Entwicklung des Judentums in Deutschland von der Macht-

ergreifung

NO-5194

ergreifung (30.1.1933 im Altreich, März 1938 in Österreich, März 1939 im Protektorat Böhmen-Mähren) bis zum 1.1.1943 gezogen werden:

1. Judenbilanz des Altreichs mit Sudetengau und Danzig

Zahl der Juden im Altreich (ohne Sudetengau und Danzig) am 30.1.1933	rund	561 000

Abgang vom 30.1.33 bis 1.1.43 durch

Sterbeüberschuß (im Altreich)	- 61 193	
Auswanderungsüberschuß	- 352 534	
Abwanderung (Evakuierung)	- 100 516	
		- 514 243

Zugang vom 30.1.33 bis 1.1.43 durch

Eingliederung des Sudetenlandes	+ 2 649 x)	
sonstige Veränderungen (Danzig, Zuzug, Wegzug, genehmigte Austritte, Anerkennung als Mischling I.Grades, Neuerfassung, Karteibereinigung)	+ 1 921	
		+ 4 570

228

Zahl der Juden im Altreich (mit Sudetengau und Danzig) am 1.1.1943	51 327

2. Judenbilanz der Ostmark

Zahl der Juden in der Ostmark am 1.3.1938	rund	220 000

Abgang vom 1.3.38 bis 1.1.43 durch

Sterbeüberschuß	- 14 509	
Auswanderungsüberschuß	- 149 124	
Abwanderung (Evakuierung)	- 47 555	
sonst. Veränderungen	- 710	
		- 211 898
Zahl der Juden in der Ostmark am 1.1.1943		8 102

3. Judenbilanz des Protektorats Böhmen-Mähren

Zahl der Juden im Protektorat am 15.3.1939	118 310

Abgang vom 15.3.39 bis 1.1.43 durch

Sterbeüberschuß	- 7 074	
Auswanderungsüberschuß	- 26 009	
Abwanderung (Evakuierung)	- 69 677	
		- 102 760
Zahl der Juden im Protektorat am 1.1.1943		15 550

x) Diese Zahl von 2 649 Juden im Sudetenland wurde bei der Volkszählung 1939 festgestellt. Vor Eingliederung des Sudetenlands ins Reich betrug die Judenzahl rund 3 . . die aber sehr rasch ohne Überschreitung einer Staatsgrenze und ohne Vermögensverluste ins Protektorat auswanderten.

NO - 5194

In der Bilanz sind die neuerworbenen Ostgebiete (mit Ausnahme von Danzig) nicht enthalten. Ihre Bilanz kann noch nicht erstellt werden. Doch gibt es über die Juden in diesen Gebieten zur Zeit der Übernahme ins Reich verschiedene Schätzungen, die auf eine Zahl von etwa 630 000 Juden hinführen dürften. Dazu kommen etwa 160 000 Juden im Bezirk Bialystok und rund 1,3 Millionen Juden im Generalgouvernement zur Zeit seiner Errichtung.x) Das würde zusammen im gesamtdeutschen Raum (ohne die besetzten Ostgebiete) Ende 1939 eine Gesamtzahl der Juden von etwa 2,5 Millionen ergeben, deren weitaus größter Teil auf den neuen Osten entfällt.

Am 1.1.1943 zählt das Reich ohne die neuen Ostgebiete, ohne das Altersghetto Theresienstadt und ohne den Arbeitseinsatz im Rahmen der Organisation Schmelt nur mehr 74 979 Juden, davon 51 327 im Altreich, 8 102 in der Ostmark und 15 550 im Protektorat. Im Altreich mit Sudetenland sind nur mehr 9,2 vH der Zahl der Juden vom Tag der Machtübernahme vorhanden. Am 30.1.1943 beträgt ihre Zahl nur mehr 48 242 oder 8,6 vH, am 28.2.1943 gar nur mehr 44 589 oder 7,9 vH. Berlin, wo schon 1880 ein Achtel, 1910 über ein Viertel, 1933 fast ein Drittel der Juden Deutschlands wohnten, zählt an 1.1.1943 nicht weniger als 32 999 oder 64,3 vH der gesamten Juden des Altreichs, am 30.1.1943 noch 30 121, am 28.2.1943 noch 27 281. In der Ostmark weist nur mehr Wien überhaupt noch Juden auf.

229

Von den 51 327 Juden des Altreichs sind 23 197 Männer und 28 130 Frauen. 40 351 sind Glaubensjuden, 10 976 sind Nichtglaubensjuden. 16 760 leben in Mischehe, in der Ostmark 4 803 (von 8 102), im Protektorat 6 211 (von 15 550).

III. JÜDISCHE VOLKSSCHWÄCHE

Die Judenbilanz in Deutschland weist einen außerordentlichen Sterbeüberschuß auf, der nicht allein durch die sehr hohe Sterblichkeit der Juden bedingt ist, sondern mehr noch durch die ausgesprochene Geburtenarmut. So hat sich die natürliche Bevölkerungsbewegung im Altreich mit Sudetenland von 1933 bis 1942 folgendermaßen entwickelt (nach den Schätzungen und Unterlagen der Reichsvereinigung der Juden in Deutschland, da die Auszählungen nach Glaubensjuden viel komplizierter und unzuverlässiger sind):

x) Ohne Distrikt Lemberg mit rund 700 000 Juden.

NC-5194

Geburten und Sterbefälle der Juden im Altreich
(bis 1939 berechnet und geschätzt)

Jahre	Geburten	Sterbefälle	Sterbeüberschuß (-)
1933	3 425	8 925	- 5 500
1934	2 300	8 200	- 5 900
1935	2 500	8 100	- 5 600
1936	2 300	8 000	- 5 700
1937	2 100	8 000	- 5 900
1938	1 000	7 448	- 6 448
1939	610	8 136	- 7 526
1940	396	6 199	- 5 803
1941	351	6 249	- 5 898
1942	239	7 657	- 7 418
1933-1942	15 221	76 914	- 61 693

Vom Tag der Machtergreifung(30.1.1933) bis 1.1.1943 beträgt
der Sterbeüberschuß der Juden im Altreich mit Sudetenland
61 693; er stellt das Ergebnis aus 14 921 Geburten und
76 114 Sterbefällen dar. Die Wanderungen einesteils, die in
den ersten Jahren fehlende und seitdem mangelhafte Erfassung
vor allem der Sterbefälle in den Konzentrationslagern durch
die Reichsvereinigung der Juden andernteils geben hier zwar
für viele Fehlerquellen Raum, doch läßt auch der ungefähre
Überblick die trotz des Rückgangs der Judenzahl etwa gleich-
bleibende Höhe der Sterbefälle erkennen. Die jüdische Sterblichkeit würde danach 80-85(gegen 10 bis 15 im europäischen
Durchschnitt) auf 1 000 betragen(im Jahre 1942).
Darüber hinaus fällt der Rückgang der Geburten auf, der dem
Rückgang der Judenzahl weit vorauseilt. Die Geburtenziffer
der Juden im Altreich würde danach im Jahre 1942 nur mehr
rund 2 1/2 auf 1 000 betragen. Ähnlich treffen in der Ostmark vom 1.3.1938 bis 1.1.1943 auf 15 188 jüdische Sterbefälle nur 679 jüdische Geburten. Im Altreich wurden schließlich im Dezember 1942 nur mehr 14, im Januar und Februar
1943 nur mehr 7 bzw.8 jüdische Kinder geboren. Es ist dabei
zu berücksichtigen, daß das Judentum schon seit Jahrzehnten
in den zivilisierten abendländischen Staaten in der Kinder-
armut voranging, wie sich an Hand der konfessionellen Ge-
burtenstatistik ergab. Der Jude Felix Theilhaber hat schon
1911 auf den daraus folgenden "Untergang der deutschen
Juden"

NO-5194

Juden" hingewiesen, der nur durch den dauernden Zustrom
ostjüdischen Blutes verdeckt wurde. Nur zum Teil hing diese
Erscheinung mit der Überalterung des europäischen Großstadt-
Judentums zusammen; In der Hauptsache handelte es sich um
wirkliche Lebensschwäche.

Bei der heutigen außerordentlichen Sterblichkeit der Juden
und ihrem Geburtentiefstand muß jedoch der äußerst ungün-
stige Altersaufbau der Juden mitberücksichtigt werden. Die
Juden in Deutschland setzen sich nach der Abwanderung ihrer
besten Jahrgänge größtenteils aus alten Leuten zusammen,
sodaß ihr Altersaufbau bei graphischer Darstellung in
Gestalt der Alterspyramide nach dem Stichwort der Reichsvereinigung der Juden der Form einer "Keule" gleicht, was
objektiv zutrifft. Es mangeln die Kinder und die zeugungs-
fähigen Jahrgänge, während die Jahrgänge der alten Leute
nicht nur verhältnismäßig zu stark sind, sondern auch rein
zahlenmäßig viel stärker sind als die jüngeren Jahrgänge.
Daraus entspringt auch z.T. die stark überhöhte Selbstmord-
ziffer der Juden, da der Selbstmord überwiegend eine Todes-
art der alten Leute ist.

231

IV. DIE AUSWANDERUNG DER JUDEN AUS DEUTSCHLAND

Die Wanderung der Juden aus Ost- nach Mittel- und Westeuropa und aus ganz Europa nach Übersee und hier wieder in
erster Linie nach den Vereinigten Staaten von Nordamerika
ist eine seit Jahrzehnten allgemein beobachtete Erscheinung.
Aus Deutschland wanderten vor allem von 1840-1870 sehr
viele Juden aus, doch nach 1870 hörte ihre Auswanderung
durch die neuen wirtschaftlichen Möglichkeiten im Reich
fast völlig auf. Dafür wanderten nun die Deutschen aus.
Die jüdische Auswanderung aus Deutschland seit 1933, ge-
wissermaßen ein Nachholen der 1870 unterbrochenen Bewegung,
erregte die besondere Aufmerksamkeit der gesamten zivilisierten Welt, besonders der jüdisch regierten demokratischen
Länder. Die Zahl und Struktur der Auswanderer wurde von
verschiedensten Seiten und mit verschiedensten Methoden zu
erfassen versucht. Doch gelangte man zu keinen einheitlichen
Ergebnissen. Die Zahlen der deutschen Auswanderungsstatistik

jene

jene der Reichsvereinigung der Juden in Deutschland und der
israelitischen Kultusgemeinden in Wien und Prag, die zahl-
reichen ausländischen Erfassungen, Berechnungen und Schätzungen, die Statistiken des internationalen Judentums und
die Zahlen wissenschaftlicher Untersuchungen weichen sehr
stark voneinander ab. So rechnete Prof.Zielenziger-Amsterdam
mit einer Zahl von 135 000 Auswanderern von der Machtergreifung bis Ende 1937, die Reichsvereinigung der Juden mit
203 000 Auswanderern. Seit 1938 ist die Auswanderung noch
beträchtlich angestiegen, endete aber fast restlos(bis auf
einige wenige Ausnahmefälle je Monat) durch das Verbot der
jüdischen Auswanderung im Herbst 1941. Die Reichsvereinigung
der Juden und die israelitischen Kultusgemeinden in Wien
und Prag kamen bis 1.1.1943 zu folgenden hohen Auswande-
rungszahlen(einschl.Doppelzählungen):

Auswanderer aus	Zahl	Zeitraum
Altreich mit Sudetenland	352 534	(30.1.33-1.1.43)
Ostmark	149 124	(1.3.38-1.1.43)
Protektorat	26 009	(15.2.39-1.1.43)

Die anfangs überstürzte Auswanderung machte genaue Angaben
überhaupt unmöglich. Ebenso dürfte das angegebene Auswande-
rungsziel, soweit es sich um europäische Länder handelt,
vielfach nur als Zwischenstation zu betrachten sein. Von
den Auswanderern aus dem Altreich gingen rund 144 000 nach
anderen europäischen Ländern, rund 57 000 nach USA, 54 000
nach Südamerika, 10 000 nach Mittelamerika, 53 000 nach
Palästina, 15 000 nach Afrika(vor allem Südafrika), 16 000
nach Asien(China), 4 000 nach Australien. Von den 144 000
nach europäischen Ländern ausgewanderten Juden gingen allein
über 32 000 nach England, 39 000 nach Polen bzw.ins Generalgouvernement, 18 000 nach Frankreich, 8 000 nach Italien,
7 500 nach den Niederlanden, 6 000 nach Belgien. Es ist an-
zunehmen, daß der größte Teil dieser Auswanderer von diesen
Ländern nach Übersee weiterzogen. Für die jüdischen Auswanderer aus der Ostmark werden folgende Ziele angegeben:
65 500 nach europäischen Ländern, 50 000 nach Amerika,
20 000 nach Asien, 9 000 nach Palästina, 2 600 nach Afrika,
2 000 nach Australien.

NO - 51 94

V. DIE EVAKUIERUNG DER JUDEN

Die Evakuierung der Juden löste, wenigstens im Reichsgebiet,
die Auswanderung der Juden ab. Sie wurde seit dem Verbot der
jüdischen Auswanderung ab Herbst 1941 in großem Stile vorbe-
reitet und im Jahre 1942 im gesamten Reichsgebiet weitgehend durchgeführt. In der Bilanz des Judentums erscheint
sie als "Abwanderung".
Bis 1.1.1943 wanderten nach den Zusammenstellungen des
Reichssicherheitshauptamtes ab:

aus dem Altreich mit Sudetenland	100 516	Juden
aus der Ostmark	47 555	"
aus dem Protektorat	69 677	"
Zusammen	217 748	Juden

In diesen Zahlen sind auch die ins Altersghetto Theresienstadt evakuierten Juden enthalten.

Die gesamten Evakuierungen ergaben im Reichsgebiet einschl.
Ostgebieten und darüber hinaus im deutschen Macht- und Einflußbereich in Europa von Oktober 1939 oder später bis zum
31.12.1942 folgende Zahlen:

233

1. Evakuierung von Juden aus Baden
   und der Pfalz nach Frankreich.......   6 504 Juden

2. Evakuierung von Juden aus dem Reichsgebiet einschl.Protektorat und
   Bezirk Bialystok nach Osten.........   170 642   "

3. Evakuierung von Juden aus dem Reichsgebiet und dem Protektorat
   nach Theresienstadt..................   87 193   "

4. Transportierung von Juden aus den
   Ostprovinzen nach dem russischen
   Osten: .... 1 449 692   "

   Es wurden durchgeschleust
   durch die Lager im General-
   gouvernement.......................   1 274 166 Juden
   durch die Lager im Warthegau.....   145 301   "

5. Evakuierung von Juden aus anderen
   Ländern, nämlich:

   Frankreich (soweit vor dem
   1o.11.1942 besetzt)..............   41 911 Juden

   Niederlande.......................   38 571   "

   Belgien...........................   16 886   "

   Norwegen..........................   532

NO-5194

Slowakei.................. 56 691 Juden
Kroatien.................. 4 927 "

Evakuierungen insgesamt(einschl.
Theresienstadt und einschl.
Sonderbehandlung)........... 1 873 549 Juden

ohne Theresienstadt......... 1 786 356 "

6. Dazu kommt noch nach den Angaben
des Reichssicherheitshauptamtes
die Evakuierung von.......... 633 300 Juden
in den russischen Gebieten
einschl.der früheren baltischen
Länder seit Beginn des Ost-
feldzuges.

In den obigen Zahlen sind nicht enthalten die Insassen
der Ghettos und der Konzentrationslager.
Die Evakuierungen aus der Slowakei und aus Kroatien
wurden von diesen Staaten selbst in Angriff genommen.

234

VI. DIE JUDEN IN DEN GHETTOS

Es sind hier zu nennen:

1. Das Altersghetto Theresienstadt, dem insgesamt zuge-
führt wurden:
87 193 Juden,
davon aus dem Reichsgebiet 47 471 (Ostmark 14 222)
  "   "   " Protektorat 39 722.

Es zählt zu Beginn des Jahres 1943 insgesamt
an jüdischen Insassen: 49 392
davon mit
deutsch.Staatsangehörigk. 24 313
Protektoratsangehörigkeit 25 079.

Die Verminderung trat vor allem durch Sterbefälle ein.
Außer Theresienstadt gibt es im Reichsgebiet eine Anzahl
von jüdischen Alters- und Siechenheimen mit kleinerem
Fassungsvermögen, die aber weder als Ghettos noch als
Evakuierungsorte angesehen werden.

 *ne - 5194*

2. Das Ghetto <u>Litzmannstadt</u> zählt Anfang 1943

87 180 Juden,

davon 83 133 mit ehem.polnischer Staatsangehörigkeit.

3. Die überwiegend in Rest-Ghettos untergebrachten Juden des <u>Generalgouvernements</u> werden für 31.12.1942 folgendermaßen angegeben bzw. geschätzt:

im Distrikt	Zahl der Juden
Krakau	37 000
Radom	29 400
Lublin	20 000 (geschätzt)
Warschau	50 000
Lemberg	161 514
<u>Generalgouv.zus.</u>	<u>297 914</u>

VII. DIE JUDEN IN DEN KONZENTRATIONSLAGERN

235

In den Konzentrationslagern erfolgten von der Machtergreifung bis zum 31.12.1942

73 417 Einlieferungen von Juden

davon

wurden entlassen	36 943
sind durch Tod abgegangen	27 347
<u>Restbestand vom 31.12.42</u>:	<u>9 127 Juden</u>

Es ist hier zu beachten, daß die Zahl der Einlieferungen von Juden größer sein wird als die Zahl der in die Konzentrationslager eingelieferten Juden, da wiederholte Einlieferungen eines Juden wiederholt zählen.

Nicht enthalten sind die im Zuge der Evakuierungsaktion in den Konzentrationslagern Auschwitz und Lublin untergebrachten Juden.

Nach Konzentrationslagern ergeben sich, untergeteilt nach Einlieferungen, Entlassungen, Todesfällen und dem Bestand vom 31.12.1942, folgende Zahlen:

NO-5194

Juden in den Konzentrationslagern

Konzentrations-lager	Einlieferungen	Entlassungen	Todesfälle	Bestand von 31.12.1942
Lublin/Männer	23 409	4 509	14 217	4 683
Lublin/Frauen	2 849	59	131	2 659
Auschwitz/Männer	4 917	1	3 716	1 200
Auschwitz/Frauen	932	-	720	212
Buchenwald	16 827	13 805	2 795	227
Mauthausen/Gusen	2 064	-	1 985	79
Sachsenhausen	7 960	6 570	1 344	46
Stutthof/Männer	28	-	13	15
Stutthof/Frauen	3	-	-	3
Ravensbrück/Frauen	1 321	531	787	3
Ravensbrück/Männer	273	44	229	-
Dachau	12 026	11 140	886	-
Groß-Rosen	231	-	231	-
Lichtenburg	195	195	-	-
Neuengamme	192	2	190	-
Floßenbürg	80	2	78	-
Sachsenburg	52	52	-	-
Esterwegen	36	33	3	-
Niederhagen	12	-	12	-
Natzweiler	10	-	10	-
K L zusammen	73 417	36 943	27 347	9 127

236

VIII. JUDEN IN JUSTIZVOLLZUGSANSTALTEN

Zu Beginn des Jahres 1943 saßen in Justizvollzugsanstalten des Reichsgebietes 458 Juden ein, die sich auf Männer und Frauen und auf Arten des Strafvollzugs folgendermaßen verteilen:

	Männer	Frauen	Zusammen
Strafhaft	350	78	428
Sicherungsverwahrung	29	-	29
Arbeitshaus	-	1	1
Justizvollzugsanstalten insgesamt	379	79	458

NO - 5194

IX. DER ARBEITSEINSATZ DER JUDEN

In kriegswichtigem Arbeitseinsatz waren zu Beginn des
Jahres 1943 im Reichsgebiet tätig

·185 776 Juden.

Davon waren eingesetzt:

1) innerhalb der Inspekteur-Bereiche der Sicherheitspolizei und des SD (ohne Posen und ohne sowjetrussische Juden) 21 659, davon 18 546 mit deutscher
Staatsangehörigkeit, 107 mit Protektoratsangehörigkeit,
2 519 Staatenlose und 487 Ausländer. Sie verteilen sich
nach Inspekteur-Bereichen(ohne Posen) folgendermaßen:

Berlin	15 100	Königsberg[2)	96
Braunschweig	110	München	313
Breslau 1)	2 451	Nürnberg	89
Danzig	.	Salzburg	7
Dresden	485	Stettin	18
Düsseldorf	673	Stuttgart	178
Hamburg	497	Wien	1 226
Kassel	259	Wiesbaden	139

1)ohne Organisation Schmelt   2)ohne sowjetruss.Juden

2) im Inspekteur-Bereich Königsberg außerdem
18 435 ausländische, d.h.fast ausschließlich sowjetrussische Juden.

3) im Inspekteur-Bereich Posen im Ghetto- und Lagereinsatz 95 112 hauptsächlich polnische Juden.

4) im Rahmen der Organisation Schmelt (Breslau)
50 570 Juden, davon 42 382 Staatenlose und 8 188
Ausländer.

237

NO- 5194

X. EUROPÄISCHE JUDENBILANZ

Der Zusammenbruch des europäischen Judentums wurde schon vor
Jahrzehnten durch den völkischen Verfall des europäischen Groß-
stadt-Judentums einesteils, durch die jüdische Auswanderung andernteils eingeleitet. Der jüdische Statistiker Lestschinsky
hat den Rückgang des Judentums in Europa im Jahre 1927 folgendermaßen verdeutlicht: "Zu Anfang des 19. Jahrhunderts lebten
in Europa 85 % und allein in Rußland, Österreich-Ungarn und
Deutschland 80 % aller Juden; in Amerika gab es zu jener Zeit
nur 2 - 3 000 Juden. Im Jahre 1925 waren 63 % aller Juden in
Europa ansässig, innerhalb der Grenzen Deutschlands, Öster-
reich-Ungarns und Rußlands lebten nur noch 57 % des Gesamtju-
dentums, in Amerika dagegen lebten 30 %, in den übrigen Welt-
teilen 7 %". Nach Berechnungen des Statistischen Reichsamts
betrug der Judenanteil Europas im Jahre 1880 sogar 88,4 vH, im
Jahre 1937 nur mehr 60,4 vH. 1943 dürfte der europäische Anteil
noch 1/3 des Weltjudentums betragen.

238

Um 1930 und in den letzten Jahren betrug die Zahl der Juden in
einigen wichtigeren Staaten Europas:

Staat	Volks- zählungs- jahr	Zahl der Juden	Neuere Jahr	Zählung od. Zahl der Juden in 1000	Schätzung vH der Be- völkerung des Wirts- volkes
Altreich	1933/35	502 799	1943	51	0,07
Österreich	1934	191 481	1943	8	0,1
Tschechoslow.	1930	356 830	.	.	.
- Protektorat	.	.	1943	16	0,2
Danzig	1929	10 448	.	.	.
Memelgebiet	1925	2 402	1937	3	2,0
Belgien	.	.	1937	80	1,0
Bulgarien	1934	48 398	1937	50	0,8
Finnland	.	.	1937	2	0,04
Frankreich	.	.	1937	280	0,7
Griechenland	1928	72 791	1937	90	1,1
Großbritann.	1931/33	234 000	1937	345	0,7
Italien	1930	47 825	1937	52	0,1

NO - 5194

Fortsetzung:

Staat	Volks- zählungs- jahr	Zahl der Juden	Neuere Zählung od. Schätzung		vH der Be- völkerung des Wirts- volkes
			Jahr	Zahl der Juden in 1000	
Irland	.	.	1936	4	0,1
Jugoslawien	1930	68 405	1937	75	C,3
Lettland	1935	93 479	1937	96	4,9
Litauen	1923	155 125	1937	175	7,4
Niederlande	1930	111 917	1937	135	1,6
Polen	1930	3 113 933	1937	3 300	9,6
Rumänien	1930	984 213	1941	302[1]	2,2
Slowakei	.	.	1940	89	3,4
Sowjetrußl.	1926	2 570 330	1939	4 600[2]	2,4
Ungarn	1930	444 567	1940	750[3]	5,8

[1] Neuer Gebietsstand.
[2] Neuer Gebietsstand, mit Ostpolen; die Zahl ist geschätzt.
[3] Neuer Gebietsstand; die Zahl ist berechnet.

239

Die Gesamtzahl der Juden auf der Erde schätzt man um das Jahr 1937 im allgemeinen auf rund 17 Millionen, wovon über 10 Millionen auf Europa entfallen. Sie häufen bzw. häuften sich in Europa vor allem in den von Deutschland besetzten früheren polnisch-russischen Gebieten zwischen Ostsee und Finnischem Meerbusen und dem Schwarzen und Asowschen Meer, daneben in den Handelsmittelpunkten und im Rheingebiet Mittel- und Westeuropas und an den Küsten des Mittelmeers.

Von 1937 bis Anfang 1943 dürfte die Zahl der Juden in Europa teils durch Auswanderung, teils durch den Sterbeüberschuß der Juden in Mittel- und Westeuropa, teils durch die Evakuierungen vor allem in den völkisch stärkeren Ostgebieten, die hier als Abgang gerechnet werden, um schätzungsweise 4 Millionen zurückgegangen sein. Dabei darf nicht übersehen werden, daß von den Todesfällen der sowjetrussischen Juden in den besetzten Ostgebieten nur ein Teil erfaßt wurde, während diejenigen im übrigen europäischen Rußland und an der Front überhaupt nicht enthalten sind. Dazu kommen die uns unbekannten Wanderungsströme der Juden innerhalb Rußlands in den asiatischen Bereich hin-

über. Auch der Wanderungsstrom der Juden aus den europäischen
Ländern außerhalb des deutschen Einflusses ist eine weitgehend
unbekannte Größe. Insgesamt dürfte das europäische Judentum
seit 1933, also im ersten Jahrzehnt der nationalsozialistischen
deutschen Machtentfaltung, bald die Hälfte seines Bestandes verloren haben.

240